Turn your ordinary into your **EXTRA**ordinary

I0161128

The Inner Millionaire

The simple step by step **GUIDE** to Financial Freedom

Andrew Barsa

National Library of Australia Cataloguing-in-Publication entry (pbk)

Author: Barsa, Andrew.

Title: The Inner Millionaire: The simple step by step GUIDE to Financial
                 Freedom / Andrew Barsa.

ISBN: 978-0-9941929-9-8 (paperback)

Subjects: Finance, personal--Psychological aspects.
                 Money--Psychological aspects.
                 Wealth--Psychological aspects.
                 Saving and investment--Psychological aspects.

Dewey Number: 332.024

Published by Andrew Barsa and InHouse Publishing
www.andrewbarsa.com
www.inhousepublishing.com.au

Contents

Contents

Testimonial

"I have been blessed to be able to spend the last 42 years of my life educating millions of people around the world on how to live more inspired, empowered, fulfilling and prosperous lives. For the last two and a half decades I have been fortunate enough to be able to specifically present educational programs on personal wealth building and socioeconomic contribution and have shared stages with many of the great leading educators in the financial field.

When it comes to educating and inspiring people on how to build their wealth and sound financial futures Andrew Barsa has certainly delivered like few others.

He has a gift, an uncanny ability to connect with his audiences and inwardly help them tap into their future success and wealth potentials. I am confident in his ability to assist his audiences in building their desired and wealthy fortunes like few others."

—Dr John DeMartini

Founder of the DeMartini Institute

International best-selling author, and consultant

Dedication

I dedicate this book to my parents for giving me life in this world. I am so grateful that I can get up every day and live the life I desire and help many people along the way.

So I just want to say THANK YOU!

Preface

The Four Killers of Wealth

So many people are in the pursuit of financial freedom and I want to share with you why they never get there.

There are four simple things that kill the chance of financial freedom, however everybody has the ability to attain it and I believe everybody has an inner millionaire inside them. The problem is that most people are ambushing their true inner gift every single day by allowing the four wealth killers to dictate their lives.

The first one being **TIME**.

Most people take time for granted and don't really appreciate how valuable it is. People only tend to appreciate time during periods of adversity or tragedy because it is in those moments that people are able to reflect and to realise that life is way too short. I'm sure you can relate to this and to remember your own personal moments of reflection.

Time has an incredible ability to heal and it can make us forget so much that the reality of life comes flooding back in, so that before we know it, we are caught up in the rat race once more. The stresses of life—paying bills, taking the kids to school or meeting the demands of your job or business take over and then we are back into our old habits and patterns.

Each day we look at the clock, wanting time to race by. The clock in the car, on the wall or on your wrist dictates the day to you. The sad part is that the clock doesn't serve humanity other than telling us the time, it doesn't tell us what's happening in our life and as each second, minute, hour, day, week, month and years go by, those are moments we never get back. The clock face has typically been fashioned as a circular face, which is a symbol of eternity and yet we need to remember that we have an expiry date and this is why time can deceive us all because it just ticks away . . . tick tick!

So with this in mind, if you are not living your life in the way that you want to and you are not doing what you were born to do, doing what you love or pursuing a life of wealth, then you are gambling your life away. To achieve and to release the true inner millionaire within, you cannot allow time to stop you; instead, you must appreciate it and value it. Where you are today in your life is based on an accumulation of time from the moment you were born until now. Where you will be in 20 years from now will also be an accumulation of time depending on what you do between now and then, so I urge you to stop wasting time and ignite that inner millionaire within you.

Procrastination is the second killer.

Procrastination derives from not appreciating time; people always put things on the back burner thinking they can do it later. Procrastination is also an automatic mechanism which is created based on a lack of belief; people who are in the pursuit of wealth will never procrastinate because they are on a mission of achievement. Procrastination is not a growth strategy. Ask yourself when was the last time you procrastinated? How has it served you? How many opportunities have you let slide because of it? Or how many times have you thought, what if?

I encourage you stop waiting for the perfect opportunity, just go out there and create it.

Incompletion is the third wealth killer.

There is a huge amount of people who are never able to finish off what they have started, they consistently look for the easy way out, they are focused on the quick buck rather than making the long term fortune. Most people will change their job or business 14 times between the ages of 18 to 40; it's no wonder that most people never reach financial freedom. Many get really close to receiving the treasures of wealth then they stop because of self-doubt. I will go into self-doubt later on in the book. However always remember—perseverance is the key.

Fear is the fourth wealth killer.

How many times have you heard that fear is the choke-hold of success and wealth?

Fear is an illusion we create in our minds, it doesn't even exist. Our mind is the best movie director in the world and it creates an image of you not succeeding giving you a perception of loss which makes you scared. People are afraid of being tagged as a failure. Allow me to show you how you can conquer your fears and allow your inner millionaire to shine.

> 66 The only thing we have to fear is fear itself. 99
> - *Franklin D. Roosevelt* -

Introduction

This book is all about the psychology of wealth and how to free up your inner millionaire. Having financial wealth isn't everything of course although many people are governed by this. The psychology of wealth encapsulates far more than this, because money is just one vital component. In my Belief System, there are four components that make up *The Inner Millionaire.*

- Emotional fitness
- Mental fitness
- Spiritual Fitness
- Financial fitness

The inner millionaire is a way of thinking, it is an attitude, certain behaviours or traits that we all have within us. It's about managing all our states, the emotional, mental and spiritual which will produce a very healthy financial state. I truly believe we dictate whether we choose to release that component. The inner millionaire is awake inside you and all you have to do is nurture it and allow it to grow. However, since the majority of the world only earns in the thousands, I call this the "thousandaire mentality", this is also a way of thinking which I believe is a limiting attitude.

Throughout this book I will be covering the behaviours, traits and way of thinking that will help you to release that inner millionaire but if you have reached financial abundance already then this book will demonstrate all the great things you are currently doing and will also provide detailed reminders of any aspects which may have been forgotten en-route.

Master the ritual of repetition.

So if we take a look at wealth as a whole, it is empowering. It is about having resources, opportunities, freedom, options, flexibility and legacy. It's about having a vision for the future and being able to manifest these invisible ideas into physical entities and being rewarded for it. Sadly, the time we spend on this planet is extremely short and so I believe that it's imperative to identify what you truly want to achieve in life as soon as possible. To ascertain this, it's necessary to dig deep within your subconscious mind, to reach that core "you" and to identify what it is that you are really longing for?

Are you looking to provide a great lifestyle for your family? Do you envisage going away on holiday, creating memories and spending quality time with them or are you searching for the celebrity lifestyle by having flashy cars, homes and yachts? Perhaps you are yearning to create a global legacy?

Whatever your ambitions are once you have identified your dreams and have actioned them, this will give you all the freedom in life you need, enabling you to live with passion.

I was born and raised in West Sydney and from the age of about 6 to 20 years old, I could see rapid and diverse changes occurring, it affected how we lived, the shift of multiculturalism, expansion in business growth, road traffic began to increase, and people were getting busier. There's no doubt that the world around me was changing fast.

I have 2 younger siblings—one sister and a brother so when I was growing up, I had a huge responsibility in looking after them. My parents were working really hard trying to support the family and so it became my responsibility to take them to school, to cook, to help deal with their school issues—which included important occurrences such as: bullying, being teased and making sure they did their homework on time.

I was raised in a middle-class family so I don't proclaim that my story is a rags to riches adventure, however, I did witness many arguments about the subject of money—including the struggle to pay the mortgage each month, the ever-increasing bills and the inability to afford everyday things.

I strongly remember returning to school after one holiday period and the teachers would gather all the students together and ask what we did during our holidays and for details of where we had gone. I clearly remember that most of the kids had been away to Nelson's Bay, Port Macquarie, the Gold Coast or the US. They all had really nice stories to share however when the teacher asked me, I really had nothing to say other than, "Um I didn't go anywhere, I played with my soccer ball in the backyard."

This made me feel quite awkward because I didn't really understand why everyone else was going away and I couldn't. So I'd go home feeling totally despondent and ask my mum why it was that the other kids at school went away to such great places and we didn't and my mum would admit that we just didn't have the money. The promise of a holiday the following year would hang in the air but as the months went by, the same thing would happen. Eventually I realised that next year would never come.

As time went by, the family disagreements about money never changed. It was tough to witness the people I loved the most constantly fighting about a piece of paper called MONEY!

Sick of the never-ending rows, I made a promise to myself that one day I would be wealthy and I would give all the money to my parents so they could be happy and never have to worry again. I also wanted to make sure that my future kids would never experience the constant rows over a lack of money.

So I tried to come up with innovative business ideas that would make me rich. I was an ideas person and I always visualised becoming an entrepreneur and running my life my way. Many times I would come home to share some of my ideas with my dad because I loved him so much; he was my hero and my idol. However, he would consistently tell me, "Andrew, it sounds good but this is why it won't work," or "You have to work really hard and you are too lazy," or, "You need to have money to make money," etc. It was frustrating. Even my friends and my teachers would say that I was not smart enough, or that in this world, you had to be lucky to be successful. I was facing consistent dead ends, feeling disheartened and sad that no-one believed in me.

I remember a specific moment in my life where I shared an idea with my father—one that I was so excited about, but yet again my father listed all the reasons why it wouldn't work, and suddenly, this made me really angry. I wanted to know why he always looked at the negative aspects rather than at all the aspects which were good.

He merely stated, "I have a lot more experience in life, you should listen to your father."

Now my story is probably not so different than for many of you reading this book and if so, you will know how hard it is to take constant setbacks, to want to achieve something in life but to feel that no-one truly believes in you. Now don't get me wrong, my father is an amazing man who made us rich in the love that he gave us. He also taught us many values and worked hard to provide for us all. He tried to spend as much time as was possible with us, but there was no getting away from the fact that money was a big issue. I also realised something fundamentally important, because money had always been an issue for him; he was consistently recalling his own bad associations with money, passing in fact, his money baggage onto me. This really puzzled me. My father was very educated, he was well-read and had a lot of knowledge along with numerous degrees; and he could also speak four languages.

So my big question was: how could one be so knowledgeable and educated yet not be financially happy?

The more I contemplated this, I became aware that this didn't only apply to my dad but to many people all around the world. I later discovered there is only one main reason for this and it starts with the power of the mind. This may sound simple, but sometimes, we miss the whole concept of success throughout our entire life because it is easy to get stuck in the box rather than to step outside of it and to view life with some clarity.

So from those very young years, I became passionate about understanding the mindset of those who are successful in life and realised that to be successful, I had to move away from the mindset of those who are not.

It is precisely this information and my own journey to success that I want to share with you now.

At the end of each chapter I would like you to write down all that you have learned so that by the end of the book you will have your own summary. Each person will resonate differently and this is because we are all unique in different ways and will need to improve in different areas.

Chapter 1

Wealth is a Mindset

> 66 If you are born poor, it's not your mistake. But, if you die poor, it's your mistake. 99
> *- Bill Gates -*

So now that you know who I am and why I set upon my journey to discover the psychology of wealth and how I released my own inner millionaire. What I'd like to do right now is to share with you, one step at a time, all of the things I discovered which will enable you to ignite your inner millionaire and live a life of abundance. You will see how the life you live is clearly about how you perceive the world through your eyes.

Over the years, I have met and worked with some of the richest and also, some of the most challenged people in the world. My biggest question has always been, why are some people wealthy and others not? This question has fuelled my waking hours and has driven me forward to discovering the truth. I soon discovered that a great many people make a great many excuses including:

- Family
- Background
- Lack of connections
- Education, etc.

I quickly eliminated these reasons because actually none of them seemed to make a difference. I had met many educated people who are rich, and lots of educated people who were financially struggling.

I also met uneducated people who had become rich, and talked with uneducated people who were financially struggling. So, the usual reasons cannot therefore really apply. After a while, I started to realise that most people actually have the amount of money they truly believe they are worth.

Note: It's not what people think about themselves because we can all say that we are great, it's about what they truly feel and believe *in their heart.*

Don't get me wrong, I'm not for one moment suggesting that an individual who is raised in extreme poverty (Third World countries) would have access to the same opportunities as someone who grows up in a wealthy neighbourhood in a First World country. So there are exceptions to the rule. But it is important to note that even in those extreme and dire situations, there are those who rise from those humble beginnings and go on to achieve greatness. There are also those who labour their entire lives for a pittance.

What it boils down to is this: poverty is actually a state of mind. It's the sum total of all the little stories we tell ourselves. Consider your own journey through life to date; have you achieved the successes you need? If not, maybe some of this is starting to make sense with you. Is there a dawning of recognition that maybe, just maybe, you are not utilising the power of your mind and perhaps are failing because you don't—hand on heart—believe that you should?

When I realised that our state of mind was the key to it all, I started to listen to everything that people were saying about money. I needed to understand their relationship to it. The more I learned, the more I became convinced that I was on to something big.

The Fox and the Grapes

I don't know if you've ever heard the Aesop fable about the Fox and the Grapes? It tells the story of a fox that is desperately trying to reach some grapes on a vine which are hanging out of reach. The fox keeps jumping but never quite manages to reach those grapes. After a while, the fox frustrated, decides that the grapes were probably sour anyway and wanders off.

This is the root of the phrase, "sour grapes". The story also serves as a lesson about our attitude to money and about giving up.

When we are children, we dream of having everything we want: planes, boats, adventures in exotic locations, big houses and a hundred other things.

But as we focus on our dreams, a strange thing often happens, negativity starts to creep in as we realise that many of the things that we want in life are harder to attain than we initially thought. We don't think just how good it will feel to achieve them and we are never truly taught how to strive for goals. Our schools and parents, unless we are exceptionally fortunate, are not equipped to teach us the mindset of wealth acquisition. So we begin to believe that these luxuries are too difficult, we start to draw up reasons why we can't have them, just as the fox decided that the grapes were sour. We do this because it means the pain of not having money is replaced with a false but comforting belief that it wasn't worth having anyway.

These little stories are echoed by those around us, and eventually they become our reality, and our prison.

In this book, I will share some of the interviews and breakthrough stories that I have been involved with and I will explain how I helped these people experience their breakthroughs, by simply listening to them and by asking the right questions. You may be thinking that this sounds too easy, how can listening to someone possibly change someone's mindset? But my role was to help them to look at their perception of life.

When you analyse your perceptions, you will be able to see how this becomes your reality. In this process, it means stripping away all the lies and misconceptions about the real nature of our reality. It's about how we really interact with people and how we limit our thinking and our achievements, because people really do not know the true power of the mind. Your mind defines your reality. When we realise that the key to success is stored within our minds, we can really see how it defines our reality or how it could hold us in bondage to a life of abject mediocrity—if we let it.

I found myself wanting people to understand that they could be free to experience so much more joy and happiness. These fundamental components shape and define you and determine if you are going to be successful and have a truly fulfilling life.

Throughout the book I will consistently ask you questions, these will be thought-provoking and make you turn your attention inwards. Once you have read this book and have answered all the questions, I can promise you that you will look at the world and yourself in a different way and this will enable you to become the master of your own life and you will realise that the inner millionaire also lives within you. Nothing is ever missing in our lives and everything is already within us because we all have the genius, the leader, the gift and we can at any given time access these attributes and apply them in our day to day lives.

My background is as a trader in the financial markets, and over the years, I have taught thousands of people across the world how to monetise the markets. Finances are the one thing that people naturally think of when they hear the word wealth and during my journey in teaching people, I discovered the psychology of the mind and how it encapsulated four important areas.

Here's a reminder:

- Emotional fitness.
- Spiritual fitness.
- Mental fitness.
- Financial fitness.

Now, how can one person take knowledge and strategy and make a fortune? How does another person do nothing with their knowledge? I had an overwhelming desire to find out how I could help the majority of my students to become successful, happy, and, to believe in themselves.

One thing I established is that it is not all about having a high IQ because this only relates to knowledge and education. Instead, I focused on something known as EQ. This stands for Emotional Intelligence.

It is the ability to identify, use, understand, and manage emotions in a positive way to relieve stress, communicate effectively, empathise with others, to overcome any challenges, defuse conflict, to change a perception of events and, to make wise financial decisions.

Once you have full control of your emotions you can see everything in slow motion. Just like an athlete at the peak of fitness, where commentators have been known to say that the athlete is so great, that they appear to operate in slow motion. The reason for that is there is no panic; no fear and they have a high level of clarity and vision. Life is sharp.

Author's Note:

I met an amazing man in the last 12 months. He was homeless and had been living in South Africa for about 8 years. I have to say that being homeless in South Africa is probably going to be a really tough gig. However this remarkable story will signify that anything is possible in life.

One day Ken was laying on a park bench trying to catch up on some sleep. He had been living out of his old busted up car so, not ultra comfortable but then suddenly another car randomly careered into his while it was parked, so Ken got off his park bench and made his way over to the vehicles, nodding to the to the gentlemen who was very apologetic. He gave Ken his business card while exchanging details and told him to go along to his office and he would give him a cheque to pay for all the damage.

Although Ken meant to collect his money, it just never happened and about six months later Ken was driving along and he noticed a name on an office building, it was the same as the one on the business card that the gentlemen had given him. Ken decided to walk in after 6 months and to ask for his cheque.

Surprisingly the guy came out and asked where he had been. The cheque for 12,000 rand had been waiting there for him. Ken thanked the gentlemen, surprised by his honesty and gratefully took his money. Tired with being homeless and having to live out of a car, he decided that he wanted to do something with his life, and to make some changes so that he could settle in his own place. Some years previously he had been involved with selling natural vitamins. Now he decided to take the approach to health and to his income much further. He went directly to a pharmaceutical company and asked if they could create a blood cleansing tablet that would help Africans especially as there are many who have HIV and other serious diseases. He said that he would invest his full R12,000 but was told that they could not do it for that amount.

Ken somehow begged and convinced them to produce the tablets. He subsequently sold them and managed to turn his R12,000 investment into R24,000. He then went to a local radio station and said he would like to promote his pills. He used all of his profit to do so but ended up receiving no business from his advertising campaign, it was a complete disaster and said he would like to promote his pills. He used all of his profit to do so but ended up receiving no business from his advertising campaign, it was a complete disaster.

Even though this was a big set-back, Ken decided to try to get another R12,000 worth on consignment and told the pharmaceutical company that he knew he could sell it but admitted he had made a poor decision with the money he'd earned previously. Somehow he convinced them to continue and Ken, then over a 6-month period kept on selling and saving until he man-aged to make R200,000. He then courageously took that money to the same radio station where he had lost his money previously and asked what they could do for a R200,000 campaign. They told him that they could do a lot for him.

From that day on, Ken's life completely changed. He was now turning over 22 million rand a month. This is what happens when a courageous man wakes up and decides to do something with his life. He took risks and not all of the risks paid off, however that didn't stop him, he decided to persevere during adversity. Some people may say he was lucky but luck had nothing to do with it, he created his own luck. There are millions of people globally who have a little bit of money or have won major prizes and did nothing with it.

I believe we create our own luck and learning how to seize or create opportunities is the key to success and wealth. My message to you is this, it doesn't matter what situation you are in. I believe, where there is a will there is a way. Don't focus on the unfortunate environment you may have been raised in but sincerely believe that you have a bigger purpose than your current environment. Ken already had the inner millionaire within him but for so many years he chose to have a poverty state of mind. He was homeless, and you may wonder how a homeless guy could become a multi-millionaire over a short period of time. Well the answer to that is that the inner millionaire was just waiting to give himself the permission to become wealthy

So let's now move onto how you can change your life, starting from the foundations up.

Chapter 2

The Power Within You

> **Celebrate your insecurities; they are the fuel that drive you to success.**
> *- Andrew Barsa -*

Do You LOVE Yourself?

It might seem an odd question to ask but you need to really consider the answer. I am not talking about being cocky and of your being so impressed with your own importance that you don't care about others.

I am talking about that moment when you wake up and look at yourself in the mirror while brushing your teeth or combing your hair. Can you sincerely look at yourself and truly love the person you are, accepting your qualities and also any insecurities?

Instilled within us from childhood is the message that we must not be self-centred, or think too much about our own greatness. We will only sound big-headed or conceited. Society and our families endorse this message to not think too highly of ourselves and as a result, it's not really surprising that people sometimes fail to reach their full potential.

It is one of life's taboos.

One of the main ingredients of the inner millionaire is self-love. Loving yourself means that you wake every day, embracing the person you are. You accept who you truly are and you greet each day with a smile and with a strong sense of purpose, hoping to make a difference in the world. No one in this whole world is perfect, but it's not about perfection, rather it's about having an accurate perception, the ability to not hold ourselves back from achieving and to really live to the full, focusing on what we are good at, and accepting our insecurities and not being chained by them.

Insecurities are great! Don't hide from them; embrace them because these are things that will allow you to live free and to achieve anything you want.

There are two types of insecurities:

- Those that paralyse you
- Those that inspire you

I will give you an example. If you have someone who is insecure about money, it has a power over them. It could paralyse them, making them hold on tighter to what they have and stops them from doing anything to change their situation. Or, it can inspire them to go out and make a difference so that they can be sure of having the amount of money they desire.

With acceptance, comes a release of anxieties and fear. It's a case of letting go of those insecurities, and to avoid feeling angry, sad or depressed by life.

"If someone is depressed because of their circumstances, they are living in the past. If someone is experiencing anxieties, they are living in the future and if someone is living in peace, they are living in the present," as quoted by the famous ancient Chinese poet Lao Tzu. Doesn't it make sense to live in the now? If you focus on the present, it will take care of the future because the present is what you can control.

We should never feel as if we need to emulate others. You don't need to be like anyone else, you can be successful in your own right. There is no need to be jealous of others either, just make the right steps towards changing your own life and you will see and feel the difference. People need to stop beating themselves up about their failings and instead remind themselves of all the positive attributes that they possess. We all have the traits of the greats and all we need to embrace the possibilities and the world around us will change for the better.

"The world around you changes when you change."

I'm not saying you should not have role models or mentors. Analysing the successful attributes of those you admire is commonsense. If it works, then don't reinvent the model. Follow the traits, but don't try to become a clone; the greatest and most successful people in life also have insecurities and a downside. They are not perfect.

So allow yourself to come out, open your heart and your soul and say

I AM GREAT!

The Power of I AM

I AM.

"I AM" is power. As such, it will free you, once you have grasped the concept fully and are aware how to use it. "I AM" is all about who you are. "I AM" is your core centre and it is about the truth and the experiences that you attach to it. It's important to be careful about the aspects that you attach to this core you. It will limit your every move or free you.

Use these statements each day and remind yourself:

I AM Pure Love, I AM Pure Wealth, I AM Total Health, I AM Pure Spirit, I AM Effortless Power, I AM Total Abundance, I AM Of Plenty, I AM the Divine Substance, I AM Filled With Strength, I AM True Source Energy, I AM Pure Genius, I AM Infinite Beauty, I AM Life, I AM Filled With Colour, I AM Thankful, I AM Of Divine Mind, I AM My God, I AM Truthfully Happy, I AM Fun, I AM My Law, I AM Open-Minded, I AM Young, I AM Wise, I AM Wonderful, I AM Filled With Positivity, I AM Determined, I AM Exceptionally Motivated, I AM Persistent, I AM Upbeat, I AM Confident, I AM Thoughtful, I AM Tolerant, I AM Filled With Integrity, I AM Confidence, I AM True Divine Energy, I AM Total Success, I AM Intelligence, I AM Truth, I AM All That Is Good, I AM That I AM, I AM Of Pure Mind, I AM Joy,

I AM One With God, I AM Perfection, I AM At Peace, I AM Whole, I AM Grateful, I AM Secure, I AM Free, I AM Consciousness, I AM Pure Awareness, I AM Mind, I AM Insight, I AM The Revelation, I AM Pure Illumination, I AM Total Enlightenment, I AM Of Heaven, I AM Unlimited, I AM True Harmony, I AM Prosperous, I AM A Magnet, I AM Gifted, I AM Responsible, I AM True Vitality, I AM Radiant, I AM Divinity, I AM The Light, I AM The Way, I AM Everything, I AM Alive, I AM At Peace, I AM Relaxed, I AM Divinely Guided, I AM Purity, I AM Noble, I AM Awake, I AM Allowing, I AM Creativity, I AM Blessed, I AM Worthy, I AM Blissful, I AM Beautiful, I AM Of Grace, I AM Focused, I AM True Kindness, I AM Pure Imagination, I AM Inspired, I AM Thin, I AM Pure Vibration, I AM The Universe, I AM Master Of My Destiny, I AM All I Desire To Be.

What is I AM?

Heavily debated by many, I AM is based upon two theories of Rene Descartes and the religious view of when Moses asked for God's name and God replied, "I am that I am."

For me, I AM is about being true to yourself. It is all about your real nature, that inner self. Only you can say I AM and mean it for you.

This is your real identity; it is the presence of your God within. I do not mean a specific religious entity. I am talking about your higher spirit. Whatever you attach to I AM, ensure that you do so with good intent and pure conviction, it will transpire in your life.

"I AM" is about your existence. Once you understand this, it gives you power. When you say "I can't do this", "I'm not adequate", or, "There is no way", then just stop for a moment, contemplate and remember who you really are. Instead, focus on the positive. Focus on the inner truth, say, "I AM THE WAY." The road ahead will open up and be filled with new possibilities.

I AM. It is your own destiny. It is your fate. If you give credence to fear by saying "I am afraid" then you are guilty of destroying yourself. Every time you feel fear and let it invade your life, you damage yourself. It is the same when you entertain jealous thoughts or negative ones. Each time you speak an unkind word to anyone, and more so if you say it aloud, you are definitely shortening and destroying your life in the process.

Negative thoughts, talk and actions only serve to break down your cells. Your body becomes sensitive to pain. Every time you say, "I am ONE," or, "I am in the NOW," you are improving your life. Every time you stand strong and refuse to be bullied by fear, or every time you follow the highest order that you know, and if you put your trust in a God, you are lengthening your life, improving your health, and importantly, you are able to make it less easy for disease to affect you.

I remember years ago when talking to my dad, he would say, "I Am Unlucky," and it won't surprise you to know that indeed he was. He certainly experienced many unlucky events in his life.

Many people say "I am BROKE, I am SAD, I am LONELY, I am NOT SMART ENOUGH," and they of course remain that way and they are killing the inner millionaire within them.

The moment you say I AM, but mean it in a positive way, you are stepping into a better future as it is an energy force that projects you forward. The moment you say I AM, you own it and all of a sudden you start to see and feel exactly what you stated. This is how the inner millionaire will be unleashed within you it is the trigger to saying I AM worthy of millions.

We are pure energy and there is no denying this fact. But where does our energy come from? It comes from the inner world that exists inside of us; it determines how you feel and what your thoughts are.

I have a quote that I live by.

"The ingredients that manifest our outcomes come from our thoughts and feelings."

Are there any times when you walked into a room and you felt the presence of someone who is powerful, happy, wealthy, charismatic, upbeat and positive and they are believable? They have an aura about them and you immediately feel a connection to them. They lift your spirits.

Or perhaps you have walked into a room where there is no energy, people are quiet, sad or negative and this immediately changes the way you feel. Negative energy drains the life out of you. Why? Because we are made of energy, we release it and we absorb it too.

To be in control of your energy, you need to control the way you feel about yourself. Does this make sense? You are what you tell yourself and you are how you act. Your physiology is a great symbol of your internal state. Happy people walk, breathe and stand differently than someone who is lacking in confidence and who doesn't love themselves.

The moment you tell yourself you are great, you feel great, the moment you tell yourself you are tired, you become tired. The mind is the most powerful tool at your disposal, use it wisely.

Just remember that you are a gift in this world, there is a reason why you are here, you were born to shine and not shrink from your true destiny. Follow the light and do not dwell in the darkness, allow your soul and spirit to live.

Note: Repeat how great you are over and over, use the list I gave you previously and remind yourself of this using the I AM strategy.

It's important that you understand how to make yourself feel in the zone consistently by remembering that you are an energy source.

Here's an exercise to start you thinking and believing in yourself:

Write down 10 things that make you feel great.

1.

2.

3.

4.

5.

6.

7.

8.

9.

10.

Once you have written your 10 items, reread them all, and then place them in order using their priority of importance, then inject this into your life more often.

I'll give an example about my strategy focusing on how to inject more positive energy into your daily life:

I love music, beaches, sport, self-improvement books, watching movies, spending time with friends, going for drives, meditation, exercise, travelling and helping others. One of the things that could bring me down is listening to the news. It's full of bad things with very few energising stories. Everywhere you go, there is bad energy. When you listen to talk back radio, to certain friends and family members, or if you pick up a newspaper—other than the sports and business section— it's all negative. All the media related services are filled with bad news.

My Daily Strategy:

Exercise, listen to music, read self-improvement books, call a family member or friend that you like and inspire each other. I plan my next holiday destination, I watch some sport and I always meditate before bedtime. Throughout the day of course, I come across negative energy but my strategy is to fill my day with so many wonderful, positive experiences that help to offset the negative experiences. This is the inner millionaire way when you have the ability to take control of your surroundings as much as possible.

Now there are certain people or events that will introduce negative energy into your life. There's no escaping it. Some of these people will be close to you i.e. family and friends and of course, you can't avoid seeing them. Don't let their negativity impact you however. We have to accept that there are others out there who wear doom and gloom like a cloak, we can still be kind and we can still like them, but for your own important energy levels and sense of well-being, it's best to minimise the amount of time you spend with them. This will help you to avoid having your energy levels plummet like a stone.

It's important to avoid looking at negative things as negative when you encounter them. Now this may sound like a contradiction but it's not, because when you experience failures, negative people or bad news, simply embrace it but ask two questions:

- Has this benefited me in any way?
- Will it benefit me?

In case this still sounds confusing, look at the following:

You are faced with a negative individual and they appear to be consistently trying to bring down your mood and energy levels albeit on a sub-conscious level, so are there any benefits?

- Are they pushing you harder to achieve a reaction?
- Have they hardened your resolve?
- Have they made you more resilient?
- Have they made you hungrier for success?
- Have they made you more determined than ever?

If you hear bad news, the benefit might be.

- That you are grateful for all that you have or for the place that you live in.
- You are grateful to be alive and healthy.

So you can see how important it is to turn negativity around. Avoid it where possible but always look to the benefits. Sometimes good things really do come out of bad experiences. Remember that life is full of experiences, good and bad, and this is never going to change. Embrace all experiences that come your way and ask yourself what you have learned or how the experience will enable you to become a better person.

Author's Note:

I remember one cold and rainy evening in London, I was on my way to watch Cirque du Soleil and the driver of my cab and I were having a great conversation about the English football league. Suddenly, he turned round to look at me and asked me what I did for a living and I told him.

He said, "Wow, you must have a great life, you are a very smart guy. Now I'm just working class!"

I could see that this guy had labelled himself and that the keyword was JUST. It meant he was minimising himself.

I asked him, "What do you mean by just working class?"

He said, "Well I'm not a smart person. I'm someone who works for somebody else, I work long hours and only get a small wage, and I'm just trying to get by!"

I asked him, "Are you not happy with the work you do?"

He immediately admitted that he wasn't.

I asked him, "Would you love to be wealthy?"

He laughed at me and said, "Yeah, who wouldn't?"

I wanted to know what was holding him back.

He said, "Life isn't that easy you know, it's really hard, plus I'm not that smart."

I queried this. "Really? Do you believe wealthy people live in the same economical conditions as you?"

"Yes but they are much smarter than me."

"What do you mean by smarter than you? In what way?"

"They are savvier. They have an education, they talk much better than me and they are good at numbers and I'm not good at that."

"Do you think they born like that or did they learn?"

He immediately said, "They are born like that."

I then asked him, "How many immigrants come here with no education and can't even speak the English language properly and yet have managed to create wealth in their life?"

He admitted that there were quite a few.

"Do you think they learned how?"

He conceded it was possible.

I then said. "So can you. Do you think wealthy people define themselves as working class or tell themselves they are not smart enough?"

He said no.

"Can you see that by defining yourself in that manner you will never give yourself the chance to live a better life?"

He started nodding and contemplating all that I had said.

As he was an Arsenal fan, I asked him if he could imagine the captain of the Arsenal team announcing they were not good enough to beat Chelsea. If he did, do you think that they would be able to win?"

He agreed that it wouldn't happen.

My final statement to him was, "You are living your life everyday and subordinating yourself with your own perception. We need to change that right?"

He thanked me for our conversation and for helping him to feel better about himself.

Sometimes, it is just a matter of seeing a situation through a new perspective.

The lesson learned is, the cab driver was never going to allow his inner millionaire to ignite and this was because of the way he described himself, "I am working class." Would you agree the moment one tags or labels themselves in that manner, they will never give themselves permission of allowing an abundance of money to enter their lives?

I encourage you if you have similar talking habits, please change it and stop killing your inner millionaire.

Chapter 3
Discover Yourself

How to be Wealthy, Happy, and Emotionally Fit

This is balance:

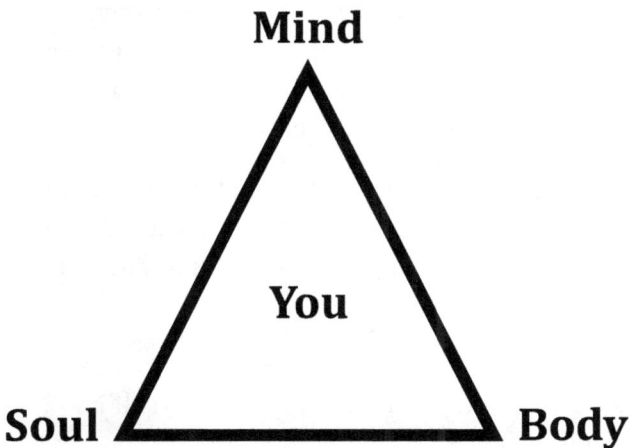

Mind

You

Soul **Body**

The mind, body and soul have to be balanced to reach abundance; it is not only about being rich even though the aim of releasing that inner millionaire will certainly change your life in a positive way. But wealth alone won't complete all areas of your life, consider those in the media spotlight who have taken their lives or have depended upon drugs to help them through. Some people can be rich in monetary terms, but not in the quality of their lives.

If you want to become rich, or "wealthy" in the true sense of the word, and financially free, before you even think about anything else, you MUST master your mind, soul and YOU. Embrace yourself each day and become happy in your own skin as this is the greatest gift of all.

So with this in mind, please write down:

How you would describe yourself?

Consider just who is the real you. No one knows you like you do, so you should be able to write down pages and pages that reiterate every aspect of yourself.

The aim of this exercise is not to keep writing down what other people might expect from you or your own perception of keeping up with the Joneses. It's about identifying who you really are and being honest with yourself. Remember that all-important I AM.

When you focus on that inner I AM, it's important to not settle with what you think is realistic. You need to look at the pure essence of your being. Think beyond the here and now, think big, it's not all about the physical either, let your innermost being emerge.

I have to admit that I initially didn't understand this at first. I thought that in order to be rich, all I had to do was to try to make as much money as possible and then the rest would just fall into place. I could not have been more wrong.

This is also the mistake of many others. I found that in order for me to achieve, I needed to love myself, belief in myself and I could only do this by knowing myself.

Why?

Well, consider this, how can you get people to love you within your relationships and even in your business connections if you don't love yourself? Similarly if you can't believe in yourself or truly know the person that you are, you will simply send out a confusing message of self-doubt.

This statement is made by many: "Fake it until you make it."

I'd like to say BE IT until you make it!

Let's make it crystal clear, just BE the person you want to become otherwise you won't make it in life, use it as a stepping stone towards your dreams. Leaders act and behave like leaders before they are given the title of a leader and an entrepreneur is behaving like one before they become a successful business person. So faking it can get you inside the designated role but BEING IT will allow you to progress much further in life if you truly believe in yourself.

People focus on the creation of goals but they forget about self-belief.

Faking it will not work long term. It is possible to work for short periods of time and to cope without knowing your true self, but you will always be limiting your opportunities, and you will find that eventually, life takes a downward turn. If you assume fake characteristics, you are only conning the true you, if you do so, it will create internal unhappiness and this why so many rich people in the public eye may look happy and fabulously wealthy but behind closed doors are in a major state of depression.

Now write down in full how you believe others would perceive you by the way you act and talk:

1.

2.

3.

4.

5.

Once you have done so, consider your comments in full. Are you surprised by some of the observations you have made? Are your comments mainly negative or positive? Were you completely honest?

I remember when I was in my late teens and early 20s, all my managers would say to me, "Andrew, you have a massive chip on your shoulder, you think you know it all and you don't want to accept constructive criticism." Or, "Andrew, you have a talent to do well however unless you are prepared to listen and to better yourself, then you will struggle in your life."

At that time, I seriously thought the whole world was against me. My family did not believe in me, my managers' were telling me I had a massive chip on my shoulder and I was refusing to listen to anyone because I thought I knew better. I had insecurities and an abundance of rejections playing over and over in my mind constantly which only caused me to rebel against authority.

I was earning good money as a young guy and still only in my early 20s but I knew it wasn't great money. There was something inside of me that wanted to earn a lot of money and I felt a real compulsion to become wealthy. But instead of approaching life in a positive way, I started to self-sabotage myself by associating with the wrong crowd so that I could escape from my perceived negative world.

I reached a point in my mid 20s where I fell into depression and, I admit, I even had suicidal thoughts because I honestly felt I was not loved by anyone. I would become emotionally attached to anyone who gave me attention.

So the slippery slope continued, I wasn't showing up to work and became lazy, accepting that my potential was not good enough. Until one day I hit rock bottom. I was only 26 years old and had $100 to my name. I blew all the money I had, I stopped working, thinking that things would be fine and somehow, I'd get that miracle opportunity knocking on my door.

The truth was I didn't even know who I was. I certainly didn't love myself and more importantly, I didn't really believe in myself. I suddenly realised that thinking I could be wealthy and actually physically doing it were two different things.

One day I had an epiphany and finally woke up to myself. I let go of the ego and pride. I had so much emotional baggage that I was carrying throughout my life and I was simply ignoring it all, hoping that it would go away without me confronting it.

I was in hell but I realised that some of the most successful people had been to hell and back many times over in order to get to their version of heaven. I began to believe that my hell would act as a trampoline, a springboard if you like, that I could use to achieve the heaven of happiness and success.

I woke up to myself because I suddenly realised I had slipped so far down the track that I had become a nobody. I was forced to get a job earning $14 an hour and I felt like the biggest loser. I had been telling everybody how smart I was and how I could do certain things, sharing with anyone who would listen about some of my past achievements but I had nothing to show for it.

I felt like a hypocrite. I was that Mr Know-It-All and I was miserable and hated my life and my job.

I knew things had to change, I knew I had to start listening more and to accept anything anyone told me—whether it was positive or negative. I would then dissect what people had told me and would try to make it benefit me in some way. I began to explore the idea that if you looked at any situation closely enough, you could take it as a lesson in life. It would enable me to be a man in control.

This is why it is important to have a really solid conversation with yourself and to break down every thought and feeling until you establish who you really are. When you consider how you describe yourself and thereafter, learn how to love yourself, then these are the foundations of greatness, because when you know the true reality of you, then nothing else matters. You stop focussing on bringing yourself down and instead, you seek achievement and improvement.

The moment I changed my own limiting perceptions, everything changed for me, the moment I realised that I dictated my world and the world did not dictate to me, then my life changed immediately.

"How one perceives the world is a clear reflection of their world."

That was exactly me.

We as humans get stuck in the **problem world**! We think there is no solution or it's just too hard. The moment you look at a problem as a question that needs to be answered then your whole perception to those problems change. In fact, you don't look at it as a problem but more like a challenge that can be fixed.

Life can be looked on as a series of questions, for example:

I have no money > what can I implement that could make me more money?

No one loves me > what kind of person do I need to become?

Everything that you see, think and experience becomes your perception in life. Your eyes become the gateway to your soul and to your inner world. I always thought that I didn't need to listen to anyone because it meant that I was weak, but my ego was controlling me and not allowing me to explore and to embrace all of the lessons in life and was in fact, preventing me to live fully.

Experience is Everything!

Life is all about experiences, some we love and some we don't, but we should still celebrate them all as they add to the rich tapestry of life.

I began to notice that the greats of the world had advisors and mentors. This made me contemplative and I started looking at the CEOs of companies, realising that they made the final decisions but they have a board of people who specialise in certain areas, these are advisors. Now if you translate this to your own life, you can equate those life experiences as your advisors but you are the CEO of your life and you make the decisions.

The results we produce in our life are merely a clear reflection of our thoughts and actions. Results are a mirror image of you.

Once you have accepted and told yourself that you are ready to experience and embrace anything that life presents, then you can look at life as a fun game of challenges and start to prepare for greatness. This knocks negativity on the head.

The next step towards success is having the Belief System.

My Belief System is called **TFBIBR**:

- Thoughts
- Feelings
- Belief
- Inspired Action
- Behaviour
- Result

Anything we look at starts off with a thought and if we consider that we are bombarded with thousands upon millions of thoughts each day, you can see that our thoughts are bound to have a huge impact on us. Whether the thought eventually becomes an idea or grows into an opportunity depends on a number of factors. An initial thought will then move into the way you feel about it.

This is where self-esteem and confidence will be measured internally. If you love the person you are, it will create an inner belief that you can achieve anything you want.

On the other hand if you don't know yourself or if you do not truly love yourself, then self-esteem and confidence will be low and this again will affect your inner Belief System.

Once the Belief System has been triggered, then this will impact the amount of action we take. Now let's face it, most people who don't love themselves, know themselves and have confidence. But they become disbelievers in themselves. This is clearly seen in the world around us as most people struggle to take action or even when they do take action, it is only marginal because of the uncertainty within them.

Now compare this to the man who believes in himself, knows himself and who oozes confidence, his self-esteem is so high that his Belief System becomes beyond measure. An individual like this takes MASSIVELY inspired actions.

Once inspired action has been taken, you need to look at your day-to-day behaviours. This is important because your behaviour determines what you will do on a regular basis and it will determine how you achieve. Compare those decisive people around you. They take action so their behaviours are likely to be determined and strong.

If someone is ready for success and they have an intrinsic belief in themselves, then they will have already taken massive steps forward, resulting in action and therefore their behaviour is working for them and not against them. They are putting in the time and have strategised the perfect route for them individually, and so they keep working at it. This is the contrast between successful people and those who never quite make it.

The last step now is to consider the actual **RESULT.**

For those who lack confidence, their results are likely to be poor. There will often be an abundance of reasons as to why they failed to succeed. But what happens when the individual has a high Belief System due to their lives feeling balanced and knowing that their inner world dictates their outer world?

Action

The difference is that they find out what they need to do to achieve positive results. They work out the strategy, they ask successful people the right questions and they invest the correct time needed. Amazingly they come back with fantastic results. This is called the **spiral affect.**

The spiral affect is intrinsically linked to having a positive Belief System. It continues throughout their lives and this is why unsuccessful, unhappy people stay stuck in a rut. They invite failure into their lives and this world becomes their reality.

To create and kick-start your own positive Belief System you need to write down 20 things that you really like about yourself and list what attributes you have already that will help to you gain success and unleash that inner millionaire within you.

Review your list daily as a reminder of your inner beauty.

Vision and Clarity

Life is a giant puzzle that we need to put together to enable us to find out just what the big picture is. The moment we identify that, we must take action, because happiness is not something we should postpone for the future, it's something we must create in the here and now.

The Power of Clarity

We live in a world that is fast-changing. We are getting bogged down in the "time is money" trap, commonly known as the rat race. However isn't it interesting that wealthy and fulfilled people operate on the same clock? How do they do it?

Focusing and developing clarity is power. What is the definition of power?

Power is the ability to make decisions and to ACT! Otherwise we become powerless.

Clarity changes everything! You know exactly what you want and this will change the way we think, feel and do at any moment. The moment we become clear, this creates focus and focus means our life will head in the direction that we want.

Happiness comes from clarity. It's that moment of satisfaction when you know that you are on track and steadily progressing towards your target. Activity will start to generate happiness. People who fail to become clear in their minds will lose track of time and they will also feel as if they are behind the eight ball, which causes them to react negatively!

In order to live the life we want, we must have vision; we must know our mission and we must ask ourselves the right questions:

What is my vision? What do I really want?

What is my mission? What is my purpose?

What specific actions do I need to take? What will happen if I don't do this?

This is something all wealthy people do and know that this is the foundation to unlock that inner millionaire.

"We are all unique and special. Born with a name that we carry throughout our entire life, our name is a reflection, a story, and a representation of who we are and become."

Treat yourself like a successful company by knowing exactly what your vision statement is, state your mission and your plan of action, and detail your forecasted deadline.

Vision

"Successful people do what has to be done; unsuccessful people do what feels good."

The most successful people in the world have passion, energy, and vision. Big visions move people. Just like the most successful companies in world, it's important to have a vision statement.

So what is the big picture? We have all at some stage put a puzzle together, but now we have to put together the puzzle of our lives. Now before we take the first step, we MUST look at the BIG picture before we match the colours or start on the edges.

So if you want to succeed you must have a vision.

Remember:

Belief is the foundation to success and when we truly believe we can do something, nothing will stop us. So when you have your reason, nothing will stop you.

The Pareto principle is the 80/20 rule, which means 80% is psychology and 20% is mechanics! Reasons come first, success comes second.

So let's look deeper into this. As psychology is 80% of what we want to achieve, we can see that it's the inner roots that dictates the fruits and, ultimately, the results we are trying to achieve.

Those firmly planted roots may be invisible but they will ultimately dictate the visible results. If the crop has produced bad results, you can guarantee that it is your inner world that is responsible for the outer world.

Why is clarity and vision important?

Imagine getting into a car and not having any idea of where you want to go. You have no destination planned, no idea what to do, so you will just sit there or drive around aimlessly. It becomes a mission impossible, and this is how so many people live their life day by day, hoping desperately that something will change and eventuate, and we all know that will never happen.

I wake up every day knowing that I must put in 100% otherwise I might as well just not bother getting up. I know by putting 100% effort into each and every day that I am going to change my life and stir up positive energy. Life will become great because greatness comes from doing the little things consistently each and every day.

"Without vision we are blind."

Whenever you have a challenge, look at the situation, visualise it, create your big picture. Create a strategy that will allow you to achieve it.

Too many people keep focussing on what's going wrong in their lives rather than considering all that is good and building upon it. Something I have discovered when talking to people is that when you ask people what they want in life, they usually give one of two answers. They will say that they don't know what they want or they will tell you all that they don't want.

The key to successful people is that they determine their goals and focus all of their energy on reaching those goals, so they become very target specific. This is why goal setting is so important.

I remember one of my clients said his goal was to own a Maserati, he was very young and ambitious and I was intrigued. I wanted to see how determined he was to achieve his goals and a few questions enabled me to see that his ambition was greatly confused with how to actually get the job done.

Here's the conversation:

"How much will it cost you to buy a Maserati?"

He replied nonchalantly by saying, "It's between 100k to 250k."

I then replied, "You will never own one."

He looked confused and asked why.

I said "If you don't know how much it is exactly, then how do you know how much you need to earn each month to be able to buy it?"

He wasn't convinced so I continued to ask him why he wanted such a car and what year model would he buy.

"How much more money do you need to earn per month to buy it and what's the difference between what you are earning now and what you need to earn?"

He seemed puzzled but merely shrugged so I kept probing:

"What is your deadline and time frame?"

And so it continued . . .

You can tell from my account of the conversation that I was pretty sure he was never going to achieve this particular dream and I'm sure you can see why. Being vague about a goal will get you nowhere. But do you have the same type of mindset?

If so, you MUST QUANTIFY your goals.

We have all heard the saying "unless you book the holiday, you never end up going". It's true. Having a target gives you something to aim at. Dreams are great but if there isn't a plan of action in place, they will remain as dreams. You must create a deadline and time will be your worst enemy.

One of my clients last year, Carel, had been unemployed for 3 years. 5 months after coaching him, he became a director of a medical company that is now expanding internationally.

His company is now turning over 150,000 USD per month and he is currently earning well over 12,000 USD per month, with projections of his business growing exponentially in the next 12 months.

The question is how does someone become unemployed for 3 years? How does it become possible for someone to not be able to find a job, to face constant rejection and to feel totally depressed? Yet, in only a few short months, he was able to completely rewire his life.

I can tell you once I removed all the mental blocks he had gained from his childhood and adolescence, it gave him clarity on exactly what he wanted. We then worked on how to create a specific strategy that would enable him to define goals. This made him responsible for working towards those achievements. It's true that the extraordinary happened.

Once your inner belief gives you permission, you can do great things. The universe will open doors for you, as long as you decided to keep knocking.

I believe in "ask and you shall receive".

I asked Carel, "What happened to you?"

He admitted he had become a victim of his world and had waited for opportunities to come to him rather than believing that he could create opportunities.

He said, "After working with you, I realised that I was tolerating an unaccomplished life and once I made the decision not to tolerate this behaviour anymore and become clear with my specific goals, my whole life changed instantly."

Chapter 4

What is Your Purpose and How Do You Get What You Want?

> **❝ Your subconscious mind is your hidden boss. ❞**
> *- Napoleon Hill -*

We have discussed previously that the first step towards greatness is to know what you want. If you are undecided, you join the millions of others who want to achieve some sort of success in their lives but don't know how. For many years, I didn't know exactly what I wanted in life either. I knew that I wanted to be happy, loved and successful financially. I also knew that I wanted to help people achieve their goals in life.

However I knew I couldn't really help anyone unless I was prepared to help myself first. How could I show love unless I really loved myself? How could I hope to understand people if I didn't know and understand myself? I was living a life of uncertainty because I was uncertain about myself. Everything we do in life is down to us and not down to our parents or our partners. It's not about our friends or bosses either.

I started to understand that life comes down to our ability to make choices and accepting the outcomes of those choices—whether good or bad. If you are afraid to make decisions and your options overwhelm you, how will you move forward?

I had become very inconsistent with my choices and my direction in life and therefore my happiness was inconsistent and my income too.

Isn't it amazing how just by being inconsistent from our foundations, it can cause a ripple-effect in the rest of our lives?

I knew something had to change, I knew I was worth much more. However, my ultimate question was how could I determine my pathway in life and find out exactly what I needed to do to find success?

Before I answer this question for you, let me say that you will always need to evolve and progress towards your goals because life is designed to do just that. Experiencing the challenges of life and filling in the gaps is a natural part of living. Remember that the moment you stop growing and discovering life, it becomes boring and this makes you feel frustrated, listless and even depressed.

What I wanted to create though was a foundation that I could stem from, and to use it as a guide for my life. Below is a technique I developed that will help you to identify what you really want and to allow your goals to evolve as time goes on. You must review this at least annually, modify it or change it as necessary.

How to Identify What You Want:

Write your own biography. Now that might sound a mammoth task but what I'd like you to do is to imagine you are no longer on planet Earth and you're looking back and reflecting on your own life. It has to be in your words and be laced with your experiences and feelings, rather than as if someone else is writing your story. What would you like to be remembered as? What achievements would you want to list? What experiences would you want to share? What legacy would you like to leave?

It's amazing how seeing your life story in black and white, and reviewing all the achievements and the disappointments, gives you a unique perspective of your life to date. It will show all those times when you procrastinated. It will also reveal all those times when you were decisive and all those successes too. It will highlight the need to create a system of action in your life if you wish to live the abundant life.

Remember that your inner millionaire is in there, it only requires you to devise your plan of action to bring it out.

Life can be tricky so what we need to do is keep it simple.

The language we use in our everyday life is a clear indication of where we are in life.

Think about when you ask someone how they are and they reply, "I'm ok," what are they really saying? If you read between the lines, you will see that it means things are not that great, or that they are simply managing to get by. It speaks volumes that their lives are not satisfying.

Now imagine when you meet someone and they answer the same question with, "I couldn't be better," or "Things are great." These words now clearly give you an indication of where this person is in life. Of course, their tone and pitch and body language will also endorse their words, giving you a clear indication that they mean what they say.

So when it comes to the roles we play in life, we can immediately change and transform the meaning, and this will change the way we feel.

When you consider your goals, consider the title too. Let's say you wish to become a stockbroker, would you prefer this title or financial doctor? What spurs you on more? In your own life, would you rather be a spouse, a soul mate or perhaps be called the ultimate lover? The words only matter if it means something to you personally.

If we look at the two images, we see a quote that I have always found extremely poignant. It states that "Healing doesn't mean the DAMAGE never existed, it means the DAMAGE no longer controls our lives".

Now this quotes sounds really nice and I can see the message it's trying to give. However, when I contemplated the meaning, I realised that I didn't like the word damage because it signifies that damage cannot be fixed. Something is broken—it is beyond repair. It's a very powerful but negative word. So, I changed the word "damage" to "experience" with the same message, it now tells us that the experience actually happened but that the experience no longer controls us.

I have shared this with millions of people around the world and asked them which one they preferred and 98% of people preferred my version because they could see how the word damage has more of an impact to one's life but how as an experience, it would be much easier to accept and move forward.

Let me give you an example, one day I was in the central business district of Sydney having a few a drinks with some friends, when I was introduced to a man who was extremely wealthy and successful. He was an Australian man living in L.A. and had spent most of his life in the U.S.A.

We started to chat and to exchange some of our achievements that we were proud of and then the conversation drifted into the psychology of success and what the real difference was between successful people and those who were unsuccessful.

I clearly remember telling him about the power of the words we use. So I decided to show him the quote and to explain to him my reasoning about the word damage.

My new friend Peter disagreed with me totally.

"I believe that there are people out there who are damaged and who will be traumatised forever. I know people who went to the Vietnam War and based on what they saw and experienced, they will never recover completely."

I couldn't dispute those awful experiences, ones that I would not wish upon anyone. So I agreed that there were exceptions but that there were also other people who had experienced Vietnam, and many other wars too, and these people had managed to write books about it and to talk at conferences or go into schools and they had begun to educate people. They had turned a very traumatic experience into a powerful message for others.

So my question to Peter was, why did some people become a victim of war and become prisoners in their own minds, when others have managed to escape from the confines of those desperate times?

I felt that some people became a victim of the experience and it became totally disempowering and the only way they could overcome the pain and damage was to rewire the meaning of their experience and change the words they use to describe it. There is power in the words. If people say they are damaged, then they will remain damaged, people will say I'm in a world of pain and they will stay in a world in pain. Peter still disagreed and then turned to me politely and said, "I say this because I am damaged."

I was surprised by his revelation but I could see he was almost moved to tears by his experiences. He had a bad childhood but I didn't want to probe too deeply as it was obviously something that had really affected him. He admitted that he had an issue with authority and that he couldn't handle being told what to do.

He had experienced 3 life threatening situations in Haiti, and while filming a movie, someone had put a gun to his head threatening to kill him. Another time he was stopped in California by the police who had pulled him over due to a broken tail light. He'd been unaware of the broken light and demanded to know why he had been pulled over.

As Peter started to pull his driver's licence out of his wallet, he began to shake uncontrollably, only just managing to hand the licence to the policeman. Feeling powerless had shaken him up. He had to admit that he was badly affected by those in authority telling him what to do.

I knew instinctively that this stemmed from a disturbing childhood experience and, to me, it explained why Peter had behaved in this way. He asked me if I could now see that he was damaged and that his experiences would always stay with him and would likely control him forever.

I asked him, "Do you love your life?"

He did.

I asked, "Do you love the fact that you have many successful businesses?"

He did.

I asked, "Are you a free man? Can you travel and do whatever you want?"

He admitted yes.

I asked, "Have you ever worked for anyone in your life?"

He stated no, he hadn't.

I mentioned that it was interesting that he had managed to work only for himself for his whole career. "Have you considered that the very fact of hating authority figures has made you the man you are today? You are a self-made, free and independent man. It's possible that if you hadn't experienced what you did as a child, then you wouldn't be doing what you are doing today."

Peter looked at me in surprise and with tears in his eyes. He had never realised that his traumas had enabled him to fight back and to become the successful person he was today. He thanked me and admitted that I had helped him to break through his barriers. I asked him if he had any sibling and whether they had experienced similar upbringings and he said that their stories were very different to his own.

I was curious. "Are they happy in their lives?"

Peter shook his head. "No, not at all. They are always stressed and complaining about their lives."

This was a revelation. "Don't you find it amazing that they had a great upbringing and you didn't and yet, you are the one who made your life successful?" I could see that he was shocked, it was a lot to digest, but I had one more question for him. "Would you trade your upbringing with your siblings?"

The answer was just as I expected—a resounding no. Peter had broken through. When he left, he hugged and thanked me. It was an amazing encounter.

One thing people need to remember that in life sometimes the most horrible things can happen to any of us but if we continue to replay those moments and not look beyond that point, we will only remain stuck fast in the darkness of our mind. For positive effect, change the meanings and the words you use every day. The inner millionaire will take a disempowering meaning and translate it into an empowering perspective.

Use this method and start looking at the role you play in your personal and professional life too. Consider all areas:

- Physical
- Emotional
- Financial, etc.

When you look at where you are in life and why, you can use the power of words to add new meaning to your being. It ignites the spirit inside us. The choice of words will affect your state of mind as I mentioned earlier with the I AM exercise.

The words I used to use before I became successful were not inspiring ones, I was always playing the victim. When something didn't work out for me, I'd play the blame game and say it wasn't my fault, the odds were stacked against me. Or, I'd just say that I was unlucky. I used to think that it didn't matter how much I tried to do something, it always went wrong anyway.

Can you see how these words can tell you so much about an individual and what their psychology is like?

How can one expect to live a life of happiness when they believe the world is against them? When I look back and reflect, I see how my whole attitude to life stunk, I could see why people didn't really want to associate with me, other than the people who felt and believed what I believed at the time. My friends, associates and those in my social networks were all losers in life, or those who at least had sympathy-seeking attitudes. I remember one day I had a female colleague ask me when I was going to start being a man and to take responsibility for my actions and the results. I automatically went into defence mode to protect my ego and pride but deep down, I knew that what she said was true.

The day I changed my choice of words, I felt that things became easier and I recommend you do the same:

- I started to say I will rather than I can't
- I will rather than I hope
- I will rather than I might

I would tell people I was feeling great when asked rather than just ok.

When I woke up everyday feeling healthy, and knowing that some people don't have that choice, I realised I was blessed just to be alive and that I still had the opportunity to create my own life and to be successful.

I implement this process with my clients when teaching them. When my clients say, "Hopefully I will be successful," I correct them and say, "I WILL become successful because I am prepared to do whatever it takes." My goal is to always remind them about the inner millionaire way.

Task:

Look at the choice of words you use in your own life so that you can change them to improve your life. Keep track on how many negative words you use without realising. Also, take a look at the words you use to describe yourself and then change those words so that they become more empowering instead. It's not easy but it is an essential part of the transformation process.

The Core Foundations

The core foundations I have covered thus far are so critical when it comes to achieving wealth and happiness, that it's imperative that you look at your basic foundations for success and strengthen those foundations if they are a little shaky. People live their lives everyday looking great from the outside but their whole existence is built upon weak foundations. This comes from their conditioning and how they deal with fear, pressure and insecurities.

Eventually the individual starts to show that they are under pressure and eventually will show signs of damage. This is why the foundations I have covered with you have to be complete AND solid within you. If you truly want to achieve wealth and prosperity in life, then you must operate from a firm foundation and one of LOVE!

The Ultimate Skill-Set

One of the most important life-skills you will ever possess is your ability to interact with people, to understand yourself and to increase your levels of communication. This skill-set will reflect all that you think about the quality of your relationships, your career advancement, the amount of money you earn, the clarity of your thoughts and your feelings about your ability to adequately communicate orally or in written form. You will be conscious of the image that you present to the world and the clarity of your goals and desires.

To lead a fulfilled life, you need a range of personal qualities such as trust, responsibility, respect, thoughtfulness, and leadership. These qualities will qualify you to develop and sustain relationships by coming from a place of service, together with your capacity to interact with people and to understand the dynamics of interpersonal relationships.

How these dynamics operate is extremely important, so that you can live a life of accomplishment.

The more that you can understand human behaviours, their traits, persona, personalities and spirituality, the more skilled you will be at appreciating the dynamics of what fundamentally drives our desires to achieve a purposeful life. The more you understand the psyche, the more you will understand how to be successful in life.

The school system that we all learned from doesn't teach us this meaningful and powerful skill-set. The ability to communicate will provide you with the opportunity to operate in a world which is underpinned and based on the exchange of goods and services and the transaction of money.

Life skills are a huge contribution to your success. It forms the foundation of your understanding of the mechanism of life and your interaction with the world at large.

Abundance

Abundance is the limitless possibilities and potentialities of the physical universe linked in perfect harmony, equilibrium and synchronicity with the universal matrix. This unified, interconnecting field of intelligence connects the whole universe with all of us. It is the universe that supplies and manifests all our needs and desires based on the energy and thoughts people project.

Whether people are consciously or unconsciously aware of its existence and its influence on their lives, the effect of this unseen force is truly mind blowing. There are no accidents; everything that happens and that will happen in your life is connected to this unseen force. It sends each of us our life lessons to help us to make a better choice, to heal our pains, and to address our unresolved issues. It also gives us all that we desire and asks but one question:

Are you the person that you have always wanted to be?

There is a saying I love:

"Hell on earth is meeting the person you could have been."

This seems to me to be very true. Nothing hurts more than missed opportunities or failing when we had the chance to succeed. People at times ask me: "Why does the same thing always keep happening to me?"

The Universe does this because it's saying that you still haven't learned from your mistakes. We are consistently being challenged and it is based on how we respond. We were created to consistently evolve and the more we grow emotionally, mentally and spiritually, the more that abundance starts to manifest in our lives. So . . .

"It's not what happens to you, it's how you respond."

Focusing every day with greater clarity is truly a blessing, a feeling of vibrancy, and it affords a healthy well-being. You will find that your mind craves clarity and purpose and service to others. Financial freedom is the outcome of what you manifest.

The mind of abundance is aware that our fears, doubts and guilt serve to paralyse our capacity to truly enjoy this wonderful gift of life. It robs us of our contentment, peace and limits our capacity to see all the good that has been laid out before us.

The mind of abundance knows that abundance is only limited by one's imagination and the goal is to free themselves of all their limitations. They seek to open their minds and hearts to experience more love, joy and happiness with less pain, fear and regret. They seek along their journey of discovery to unlock the greatness within them and to elevate their worthiness so that they can truly deserve more abundance in their life.

Once you realise that all the wealth of the world has not changed, it simply circulates and is acquired by those who can possess and manage it, you will start to see your way within the world. Your purpose is clearly to acquire the skills necessary to properly manage wealth. Money—despite all our imposed expectations and beliefs—has no personality and plays no favourites and simply moves to those who believe that they deserve it. Abundance simply has waited patiently for you to transform your image and your current reality of limitation to embrace all that life can offer you.

Patterns, Habits, and Behaviours

All patterned or programmed behaviours are a result of thoughts, ideas, values and beliefs. Our behaviours, beliefs and habits can be changed or modified. This includes your beliefs on worthiness, lovability, what you deserve in life and your wealth. Your unconscious patterned behaviour is drawn from the values and meanings that you have attached to your life experiences. The meanings you attach to your experiences and certain events will create support stories and references that produce consistent programmed responses.

Where the meanings assigned to these beliefs are found to be either incorrect or false—i.e. all men cheat and just want one thing, or generally new interpretations—you can see how you create an empowering meaning. But disempowering these meanings will trigger an entirely different response which over time will then create an entirely new patterned behaviour, i.e. I want to meet someone nice to share my life with.

This meaning is much more empowering and the universe will open up the opportunities. It's important to remember that what we focus on expands. Rather than being close-minded and condemning, it will create a behaviour that is more open, non-judgemental and friendly.

The words we choose to use creates our behaviours and repeating the same behaviours overtime will create habits. Habits will subconsciously create a program and it will operate on autopilot, i.e. I don't want to go out, it's not worth it, I never meet anyone I like.

The creation of a completely new set of experiences with a different set of assigned beliefs provides an alternative meaning in determining behaviour, i.e. I really enjoying going out because I am meeting interesting people. The more empowering meaning is held over time by the individual to be beneficial, these new experiences will become the preferred new programming mode which automatically creates a different and more positive behavioural pattern, i.e. a belief that I cannot save money changes to it's been wonderful over the last 6 months, I have saved $100 each week.

On a conscious level, self-will can override internal programming provided the person's strength of conviction and rigid determination. The mind literally reconfigures the brain's neural pathways to create new response patterns until a new habit is formed and set in place new automated behaviour responses, i.e. I now do not smoke, and want to be healthier. Alternatively conscious auto-suggestion at the level of the Alpha Brain Wave state can introduce instructions to establish new programming behaviour where there is a perceived deficiency, for example: I am an excellent communicator or I am an excellent leader.

Patterned behaviours are the programmed automated responses of the mind. The mind accepts these beliefs as fundamental truths and unconsciously, with no conscious direction, fulfills the programs that are already in your unconscious memory. The mind will literally manifest all your needs and wants including what you want to program on wealth and abundance.

If you want more you need to reprogram the mind that you deserve more:

- Why do you deserve more?
- What are you tolerating that you want to change?

Self-Worth

Those that find it difficult to save money generally may believe that they are unworthy and undeserving. Money in their eyes is an external metaphor for love. Those that do not have it at some level do not truly love themselves. Those that have it in abundance are driven to acquire money because they have placed a high value on their worth and fundamentally feel that they deserve to have what they want. Alternatively, in some people, its acquisition becomes compensation for low self-esteem and thus money is simply a tangible substitute to feel secure; the more they have, the more secure they feel. Your level of worthiness is a decision made by you and only you. It was based primarily on your perceived level of love that you received and the acknowledgement and acceptance of your existence during your childhood through to your adolescence. If your childhood was a difficult one, this may be why you have an unhealthy association with money.

This level of worthiness has determined your fundamental belief in what you deserve and moulds the very self-image which you project to the world. This image shapes how you perceive the world and how the world perceives you. This image predetermines your success in life, the quality of your relationships, your monetary worth, the perceived level that you are loved and the level of your happiness. Though the term worthiness is applied broadly, people have varying levels of worthiness in the primary areas of their life, namely health, vocation, relationships, mind, social standing, spirituality and finance. In each area, you can transform your levels of worthiness by creating a new paradigm of belief with new experiences. The accumulation of those experiences replaces the values you have assigned to your current beliefs. Change your beliefs and you change your mind's image of yourself and how the world will value you. To change your level of worthiness you have to change your level of self-belief in your capacity to deserve, in other words, to modify your self-image. This capacity to deserve is reflective of two aspects in your psyche. The value you place on your importance and the level of self-love. Your level of importance is the level that you have acknowledged your own existence. The level of self-love is the level you believe you love, care and value yourself.

This was derived from your beliefs regarding the level of love you received from your primary relationships. So, this is the perceived degree to which you think they valued your importance and the degree to which you think they cared for you. Thus, your level of worthiness is what you believe you are worth and though you think it was assigned to you from your experiences, in reality it was you who made this interpretation and determination of your value from others. Similarly, as you did previously, you can determine a different value whenever you desire, based on creating entirely different beliefs and behaviours for yourself. Our beliefs are drawn from a complex array of experiences, assigned meanings, and our perceptions of ourselves and the world together with the opinions and attitudes of others. The reason why one person is successful and another is unsuccessful draws from a variety of functions in their life. This is the fundamental reason why the course to undertake a holistic approach to wealth creation and to address the intrinsic causes and reasons for the perceived lack in your life is of vital importance. It endeavours to set the proper foundations in your mind, and then you can confidently lay your bricks of wealth creation one at a time with a clear expectation to create the life you want.

Gratitude is an expression of thankfulness, gratefulness and heartfelt appreciation. It is an acknowledgement of a perceived benefit that has been given or will be received. Gratitude transcends any indebtedness for aid, good service or kindness. It is freely given as a sincere and touching compliment of warm, loving appreciation. Your gratitude-like forgiveness was always meant for you. It is another word for love that lays dormant and serves no purpose until given away. The more you are grateful, the more you will love what is happening to you in the world.

This world is your mental reality. It simply reflects what's happening in your inner mind. Your level of gratitude and love that you see is the same as the level of gratitude and love you give out. Gratitude is an expression of self-love. Being grateful is to genuinely love yourself. It is like giving small parcels of joy wrapped up in tender kindness so that it can be returned to you with love. Those that are grateful literally have wonderful lives. They are warm and friendly and see the positive side of every situation. They have a wonderful generosity of spirit and have a mind of abundance which attracts more abundance into their life.

If you want to balance in your life and to free that inner millionaire, show the universe your gratitude for all that you have and all that you hope to have, and you will ride the roller-coaster of life with ease and enjoy a happy contented life.

The Importance of Self-Esteem

How you feel about yourself affects your whole life. Your responses to any of the many events that will occur over a period of time are most certainly shaped by your self-image so in this case, it is clear to see that low self-esteem is the key to failure and high self-esteem will be the key to success.

Self-esteem has two components:

1. The feeling of personal worth
2. The feeling of personal capability

It's easy to understand how a high self-esteem can make you feel better about everything in life but if we look at low self-esteem, it really can make people feel uncomfortable as "an individual". This may sound dramatic but it's true. If everyone could enjoy having a strong sense of confidence and a high level of self esteem, it would be far easier to achieve true happiness. Sadly many people fail to achieve this because they feel inadequate and are plagued by self-doubts and guilt, and in many ways feel that they are not enough in themselves. This prevents them from fully participating in life.

Have you ever felt as if you were on the peripheral of life and just looking in? It's a horrible situation and leaves that individual feeling empty and less than confident.

Self-esteem can be dented on so many levels. It doesn't take much for negative and critical comments to chip away at the protective veneer and for the individual to begin feeling less than whole. Low self-esteem can also turn to self-loathing and it's a slippery slope from then onwards. So in simple terms, it makes sense that everyone should start cultivating their self-esteem because those with higher levels of self-esteem are far better equipped to cope with any problems that life throws in their way, they are also far more resistant to pressure.

It's true that when you feel good about yourself, you naturally become more ambitious and that doesn't necessarily mean in a career sense, it could mean in emotional terms or simply, personal goals. When you have high self-esteem, you are less likely to form relationships that are negative and destructive in nature, remember that we attract people that match our own feelings. So if you feel negative about your life, the chances are you will only attract others who are feeling the same.

We are what we think. If we are used to poor relationships and having no money, then we attract others who feel the same. This similarity leads to a sense of familiarity. It's comforting. Then we congratulate ourselves on finding a "like-minded soul" when really, the sky is the limit in terms of achievements.

It's important to stop worrying about what others think of you. Instead, consider what you feel about yourself but don't do so from a negative viewpoint. You are unique, you are special and you are important. When your self-esteem is low, you can feel like an impostor in your own skin and it drags you down.

"The reality you see is an illusion which has been pulled down in front of your eyes to blind you so that you cannot see the truth that it is a prison of your mind. You think this is real and it holds you as a slave to its bondage. It is only when you believe that you can lift the veil in front of your eyes, you discover it was you that placed all your fears and limitations on yourself. I can guide you to the path of freedom but it is only you who can step on it."

The Law of Reciprocation

I am a great believer that what you put out is exactly what you get by return. Humans are a source of energy and it's these energies that attract each other.

Doesn't it amaze you that it's the same people who always end up in fights at the local pub?

It's always the same people who say I'm not lucky too and they become the unfortunate ones, telling you how many unlucky incidents they have experienced.

Then you have the individuals who have the ability to turn everything they touch into gold.

Have you met or do you know someone who has the ability to allow money flow into their life?

Asses their behaviour, what do you see? Is there a high level of belief? Do they have an aura or energy that says "I know I can make money"?

"Energy is contagious."

Have you heard of sympathetic resonance? **Sympathetic resonance** or **sympathetic vibration** is a harmonic phenomenon. Do you know that if I place 20 pianos in a room and I pressed the C chord on one of the pianos, the vibration of that sound will trigger all the other 19 C chord strings in the room without having to press any other key?

What this does is to tell us that energy and vibrations appeal to and trigger each other into action. This is why you see successful people surrounding themselves with other successful people, you see rich people associating themselves with other rich people and the most challenged people associate with other challenged people.

It's impossible to have a highly driven, positive open-minded person associate with a lazy, negative and cynical individual and the reason for this is there would be no chemistry; they are both operating on different frequencies. I believe your thoughts and feelings attract certain people around you that will be compatible to your values.

Never Get Comfortable

The genius Albert Einstein always said, "Once you stop learning you start dying."

As human beings, we are not created to become comfortable, in actual fact some of the most wealthiest and successful people thrive on uncertainty because it pushes them beyond any limits. It's a part of our DNA to continue to evolve and when you access the human mind and body, you can see that it is made up of 80% water so it's easy to understand the importance of water and to remember that water is in a constant flow as it spirals from the mountains all the way to the sea. If the flow of water were to stop in a pond, it would stagnate and we would see fungus, disease and insects. The lack of oxygen kills it; this is why people should continue to be mobile physically and mentally. Comfort in my eyes is the biggest killer to wealth or success.

Let me give you another example: I look at fire as being a metaphor of love and when people first get into a relationship, the love or fire is so hot, it's huge, roaring and powerful. However, as time goes on, people start to become comfortable with each other. Now the problem with this is that it doesn't matter how large the fire is, if you stop fuelling the fire it will eventually die out. This is exactly like love in a relationship; you must continue to feed it, which explains why many people lose that affection overtime and their relationships end up in divorce.

People should consistently reassess their goals on a monthly and yearly basis to eliminate the possibility of comfort. Personal, relationship and financial goals should always be reviewed because when we become comfortable with a process, we end up developing blind spots in our life, because routine is constantly the same. I have a friend of mine who one day was driving to an appointment in a location she had never been to before, and was relying on a navigator to get her to the appointment. On her way there, she was almost involved in a big car accident simply because she had forgotten to check her blind spots when merging into the lane.

This of course frightened her but I wanted to know why she didn't look over her shoulder to see if there were any oncoming vehicles and by asking a few questions, I ascertained that she only ever drove to places that she knew well and that this had been her normal behaviour for years. I considered this interesting and quite revealing because when we drive a car for years, we subconsciously drive without thinking about the actual process—in comparison to how we focused on every aspect initially.

However with my friend Lauren, she had developed a habit of not looking over her shoulder because for years, she only went on established and very familiar routes. Being complacent and comfortable could have been fatal in her situation; this is how we develop blinds spot in our life via habit and comfort.

Nothing was ever taken, missing or absent. All the skills you ever need are already inside of you, the real purpose of your journey has always been for you to find it within you.

Let's Look at Samuel Walton

This American entrepreneur, who built a small grocery store turned it into the giant Walmart supermarket chain and amassed a fortune of over $23 billion, grew up during the Great Depression.

Let's consider the first paragraph—this is a man who was raised during one of the toughest times in modern history where international trade plunged by more than 50%. Unemployment in the U.S. rose to 25%, and in some countries rose as high as 33%.

The Great Depression was a severe worldwide economic depression in the decade preceding World War II. The timing of the Great Depression varied across nations, but in most countries, it started in 1930 and lasted until the late 1930s or middle 1940s. It was the longest, deepest, and most widespread depression of the 20th century (Wikipedia reference).

Now, it would be fair to assume that most people looked at this time as the end, there was no hope and probably wondered if they were going to ever get out of this. They probably thought it would be impossible to see the good days again and could come up with million excuses as to why they couldn't be successful.

Did you know 55% of the fortune 500 was founded during the Great Depression?

The inner millionaire mindset would say: this is not the end, it's the beginning of a new era. If there was going to be a time to take advantage of very little competition to start a new business then that was the moment. It is only during times of adversity that you will see the inner millionaire shine. This is why being raised in tough conditions doesn't mean you cannot create an empire, it just means you need to think differently, to be different and not buy into the herd mindset.

Sam Walton had numerous chores to do in order to make financial ends meet for his family, as was common at the time. He milked the family cow, bottled the surplus and drove it to customers. Afterwards, he would deliver Columbia Daily Tribune newspapers on a paper route. In addition, he also sold magazine subscriptions. During his college, he worked various odd jobs, including waiting tables in exchange for meals. After graduation, he joined the US Army during World War II. After the war, he left the military and started managing a variety store at the age of 26 (Wikipedia reference).

Again Sam displayed the inner millionaire mindset. He was prepared to do anything and to not be a victim to the economy; Sam took his life into his own hands, People all over the world need to understand that you need to hustle every single day and keep pushing yourself, going above and beyond; where most people would give up and stop, instead you keep persevering.

Sam obviously had sheer determination and discipline but I believe once you active the inner millionaire within you, determination and discipline becomes second nature because you are pursuing a definite outcome, working towards a big dream, a big vision with a deadline.

He took a loan to buy his first store, and thanks to simple innovations in business, he soon bought his second store. Within 3 years, his sales volume grew to $225,000. The first true Wal-Mart opened on July 2, 1962 in Rogers, Arkansas. The rest is history. Forbes ranked Sam Walton as the richest person in the United States from 1982 to 1988. At the time of his death in 1992, he had 1,960 Wal-Mart stores, employed 380,000 people and clocked annual sales of about $50 billion (Wikipedia reference).

As you can see, Sam took the risk of getting a loan and had the belief to go out and execute. In my eyes, it's all about what you do and not what you say. That's the inner millionaire way.

Author's Note:

Your reality is a blank canvas on which to place your values and beliefs. The world simply mirrors the same values and beliefs back to you in every experience. At the point of its recognition is the point of transformation. At this point, you are aware that you alone have created your own reality and you alone are responsible for your life. It is only at this point you can take ownership of your life and then look to transform your life for the better.

I am now very thankful for all of my experiences with my father and for all I endured throughout my life. Even though I didn't like some of the experiences, they still taught me so much about life. My childhood experiences were not deliberately there to hurt or to prevent me from achieving; the opinions of others simply come from their personal experiences and perceptions. My experiences have made me the man I am today, it created a successful person who is determined, hungry to achieve and a man who wants to make a difference in the world. I understand what it feels like to be an underdog and to not have many people believe in me.

So I say this to you, always remember that you are amazing, always remember that you are unique and you are your own person—capable of achieving anything.

Chapter 5

The Power of Conditioning and
How it Can Affect You

We are conditioned to live our lives in certain ways, did you know that? All the things that happen to you, all of the experiences and events, behaviours and reactions that are witnessed are usually absorbed, without question. You start to become conditioned to believing this is how to act. Of course, no one makes you act in a certain way, but it's hard to refute lessons learned when young. You believe your parents, you believe your teachers, you believe your peers, there's no reason generally to consider that some information is less than healthy and may even be tainted. But as you grow up, you use those memories and behaviours as signals; they become instinctive responses to life's events, in fact, they form the path upon which you travel.

You may feel that no one has really influenced your behaviours, but if you cast your mind back, you will discover situations which would have highly influenced the way you make your decisions in life now.

Being a parent is hard. Most parents are desperate to protect and love their offspring, but parents aren't perfect. What if you had a father who was unable to keep a job down? Or imagine how difficult life would have been if your father had job-hopped, never staying more than a few weeks or a few months in one place of employment. If he had just upped and left, imagine the fallout from this.

As a child, no doubt you would be partially protected from the repercussions of such behaviours but even so, you would have been instinctively absorbing those behaviours nevertheless. Everything that you witnessed consciously and sub-consciously would have become part of your conditioned responses. In our example situation, your mother would have done her best to cope, but the situation would have been tough when the inconsistent and unreliable pool of money started to dry up. There would have been real issues. How she dealt with such a situation would have in time become ingrained into you.

Although you learn from your own experiences, there is a lot that is learned subconsciously through witnessing the behaviours of others, especially as a child at such an impressionable age when you absorb life's little lessons like a sponge.

When you start considering other people's behaviours and the impact it may have had on you directly, you have to consider the outcomes and of course the triggers that make those behaviours happen in the first place. In the example, perhaps your father and mother fought consistently over money, or perhaps they simply became bored within a job role after a period of time and then looked for excuses to walk out. They may have had problems with authority and being told what to do. There are always reasons for behaviours.

Parents, like everyone, have conditioned behaviours. Your father may have been acting on examples that he witnessed growing up, your mother might have experienced similar examples from her parents and have come from a background where money was never guaranteed or enough. When a parent acts unreliably and it affects the standard of living, children adapt but a lack of money and living from day-to-day can easily become the norm. There are hardships to face; you lower your expectations for nice presents or even tasty food. Life becomes basic. Although money in theory shouldn't make the world go round, it does of course, everyone needs money to be able to fund the lifestyles that they want.

Let's face it, no one wants to be short of money. You know deep down you deserve more, or at least you should, but it's true to say that sometimes we struggle and find life hard because of our actions and often because of our pre-conditioned behaviours. If being poor as a child was your reality, then it's hard to develop a positive association with money when you are older.

So, if you agree that you have been conditioned by those around you to some degree, it's important to think about how you want to progress with the rest of your life from this point. Do you want to break free from any pre-conditioned behaviours? Think about this carefully, especially if they are holding you back and preventing you from achieving all that you should.

It depends on this next answer of course. Are you happy with your life as it is right now?

If your answer is no, then why?

Consider your options. If you are not truly happy and life is an uphill struggle, forget the lessons learned previously, you have to embrace a new way of living. If you don't change, you continue to carry other people's beliefs with you. Why not live by your own standards?

Task:

Think back to your childhood years and try to recall any events that transpired that might have shaped you into the person you are today. What were you told? How did you interpret the behaviours that you witnessed?

Try to think of up to 3 individual occurrences and then once you have written them down, consider the implications of those actions, conversations or experiences. Were they powerful enough to have made you act the way you are now?

1.

2.

3.

Scenario:

Let's introduce Dave, who as a result of his own experiences, gave up on his true potential through fear:

Dave was fed up in his job, it had little in the way of opportunities and he could never rise above his current position. He had a great opportunity to work for a different company, but it was a leap of faith. He knew it would be a pressured environment, but there was a potential to earn big money. After tentatively making the decision, Dave realised that he was struggling. The pressure was grinding him down and he wasn't used to working to commission and deadlines, so found that he was not able to reach the targets that had seemed so easy initially. He felt depressed and began to lose confidence. He also started to regret leaving his old job and was unable to embrace the potential of this new role.

After some weeks, Dave gave up. He went back to his old job and within a very short period of time, was back to feeling unchallenged and bored rigid. He didn't want to accept that he'd missed out on an opportunity but because he had left without facing his issues and rising above his fears, this was exactly what had happened.

Dave never once considered whether going back to his old job was right, or if he could have used his skills more effectively by setting up his own business or even retraining in a new line of work. Fear held him back from making any new opportunities or from learning from his mistakes. There is always more to life than working for others, but it requires a certain mindset to take the opportunity to give it a go and to consider your own potential from all angles.

It's perfectly natural to doubt your abilities and to feel a twinge of fear if you are in a stressful environment that challenges you to use skills that are new to you. In life, we invariably use our existing skill-sets and experiences to prepare us for future hurdles. In principle, we can pull back from any situation, identify the skills that are needed and can tap into any memories that may be similar, using skills gained through a personal or former understanding of the situation. This is a comfortable position, when recognition of an obstacle enables an easy ascent over it, because life has placed a similar challenge in the way before. Fear will always get the better of you unless you learn to channel fear as the driver to allow you to breakthrough.

Life isn't about taking the easy way out; life is about embracing the challenges in the pursuit of success.

Re-Conditioning

You can be anything that you want to be in life. Isn't that an amazing thought? It's true though. You can have financial security, you can have success, and you can have the status that you require, happiness too. The only person who is really standing in your way is . . . you.

Success comes in different packages. Some people want money, some want status, some want love and laughter, others want a combination of them all.

I believe success is in the eye of the beholder; however my personal definition is being happy and having a balanced life, and for me that means spending quality time with family and friends and having the ability financially to do what you want, whenever you want.

Remember your millions live with you. At any given time, you can achieve whatever you want; it just comes down to deciding.

Task:

Consider your skill-set and qualities but be honest. If you are a hard worker, methodical, forward-thinking or a great problem solver, then don't be shy, write them down.

Write down as many attributes as you can think of:

1.

2.

3.

4.

5.

It is sometimes hard to write down all the positives about yourself, after all, from an early age we are conditioned to not appear big-headed. But what is wrong with saying out loud that you are good at what you do? Shout it from the rooftops if you want and if it helps you to embrace greatness.

Everyone has strengths and weaknesses, that's a given.

But when you think about the word, weakness, it's a very negative way at looking at less than polished strengths. No one is perfect and there will be areas of your personality that need to be improved, but if you let fear, self-doubt and old conditioned behaviours hold you back, then you are doing yourself an injustice.

If you allow yourself to relish all of your many qualities and to contemplate all of the skills and the passions that you have in life, along with your many talents, it is like giving yourself the keys to the door, enabling you to open up a wondrous view of the world or like shutting the door on your old way of life, eradicating those negative behaviours or false perceptions.

Never place limitations upon yourself, instead discover your true potential.

Of course it's easy to talk about releasing any negative conditioned behaviours, but to do so, you have to realise what conditioned behaviours you hold. To truly do that, you need to look at your current behaviours and consider where they came from.

Many people have been told that they are not good enough to achieve anything. They don't possess the required skills, or if they come up with new ideas, they are squashed immediately because others believe it cannot be so easy to create business ideas with true potential.

One of my clients was working for a major corporation and her boss kept on telling her that she wasn't sufficient for the role, he would tell her behind closed doors and often in front of her fellow colleagues. Sadly, Karen actually bought into his words and started to feel less than adequate. She ended up second-guessing herself and making more mistakes as a result. This shows how the power of words are so infectious to people. The words you tell yourself or the words other people tell you, can enlighten your day or bring your emotional state down.

Remember this: the words of others are only opinions.

Albert Einstein was told he would amount to nothing, Michael Jordan was told he wasn't good enough and was dropped from his college basket ball team, Oprah Winfrey was told she wasn't made for TV, and Walt Disney was told that his stories are boring and not creative at all.

The words people tell you mean nothing unless you allow the words to reach and impact you. What normally happens is that your logic becomes muddied by your past. Letting go of bad behaviours doesn't mean you are a bad person or incompetent, instead it is far more about understanding why you act in a certain way or why you might not be successful yet and changing it.

For example:

- Why did you hold back from applying for a job promotion?
- Why haven't you started the business of your dreams?
- Why aren't you earning good money and why can't you manage the money you have on a monthly basis?
- Why do you fear failure?

Once you understand who you are and where your ideas come from or even whether they are right, you will then be able to let go of those preconceived ideas that could be limiting your potential right now. Keep all of the good stuff of course, but let go of the areas that are not useful or wise.

Facing Fear

At the moment, there is a current train of thought in schools that children should be less competitive, just in case they fail and become upset by the experience. But success and failure go hand in hand. The fear of failure drives success. Being competitive and rising to the challenge is a great thing, but being able to accept defeat is necessary.

This silly and unrealistic way of thinking often comes about through the desire to protect children from making mistakes and failing. But it's impossible to stop people from failing; in fact, it is how people learn to respond to failure that can truly make them a success. If people don't learn how to react when they have made a mistake or if they have failed at something, how will they ever learn to re-evaluate, consider and plan new processes? It's important that they pick themselves back up and overcome this sense of failure.

Isn't it more important that people keep trying and striving forward than worrying about failure?

It's true to say that overcoming obstacles can be empowering.

There is nothing so satisfying as dealing with a difficult situation and coming out on top. No one wants to face a difficult time, but having a positive mental attitude such as, "I can deal with anything that comes my way," will make you be able to deal with anything. But if you are scared to take risks, or if you don't learn from your mistakes, then life can be incredibly dull, stagnating and limiting.

Who wants that?

Think back again to your own childhood and how you were taught to deal with failure? Most parents will try to protect their children, it's understandable, it is what parents do, but well-adjusted parents know that you can't go through life without making errors or failing. Parents, if they are sensible, will encourage their children to try new things— whether it is a sport or craft or a new line of study. If a child has numerous and potential entrepreneurial ideas, they should always encourage this potential, even if those first ideas may not have longevity, it's the act of idea generation that should be rewarded, of that child having the confidence to think outside of the box.

Life is filled with successes and failures. If you fail in life, it is how you pick yourself back up and progress that is significant, not whether you fail. If a teenager fails at an exam and the success of his or her future career depends upon the pass rate, then there are two choices:

- Give up and accept the fail
- Study harder and prepare to re-take the exam

The second option is what most people should do, but sadly, is not always the way. People give up because studying and retaking an exam is time-consuming and too hard. So, at that point, their dreams are shattered and they learn to accept second best.

But is it as satisfying?

Giving up at the first sign of failure is often a learned behaviour. Winston Churchill said, "If you are going through hell, keep going."

Think back if you may have witnessed a parent or sibling displaying that "it's too hard" attitude. If so, it's easy to see why you may follow suit. But behaviours can be learned just through experiences too, so the impressionable teenager who failed at an exam may have had their first bitter taste of disappointment and failure, and is now at a crucial crossroads in their life. If they choose the wrong route, it can impose limitations on them going forward and potentially for the rest of their life. Their resilience to failure at this point will depend on their early learned behaviours.

Unfortunately, people are also labelled in life.

Those who go to private school and who have families with money are often expected to achieve. They may go to better schools, have extra coaching and there is more money for decent books, they will wear their expensive uniforms with pride and be adorned with the latest gadgets. Their expectations are set higher usually as their families are successful. While this does give those with a secure financial background more opportunities, it doesn't mean that they will excel.

In the same way that someone from a housing commission background who has gone to a secondary school, but who has had less coaching, less cash, less extracurricular activities would not be expected to do as well, but they still can. Because it depends on their determination, their drive, parental support or successful role models and, whether they have less pre-conditioned behaviours which could hold them back.

People are labelled, and often incorrectly. How much better though to tear off those labels and to rip them into shreds?

Task:

How do you deal with the challenges in life? Are you someone who hurdles obstacles or do you sigh despairingly and give in, looking for the next easy option? Think seriously about the times when you have faced obstacles or extreme challenges and write down what the challenge was and how you dealt with it:

1.

2.

3.

Writing down your thoughts about your personal experiences can bring that memory and situation vividly back to life. It may be an unpleasant memory, especially if you didn't handle it well at the time. But this exercise isn't to make you feel bad about yourself, it's about getting to know the real you, the one who may be partially hidden and who just might be, at times, overwhelmed by life.

So if writing down your thoughts helps to bring them to life, then contemplating them, understanding them and considering how you might learn from that particular situation will turn it into a positive scenario now, irrespective of how long ago the situation actually occurred. This is actually a neuro-linguistic programming technique known as reframing. It's extremely powerful and enables you to view a "difficult" situation as if watching a film and seeing the situation play out from a safe distance. This distance enables you to analyse without the same emotional pull. You can use this to view your actions or decisions made at the time and to consider if there were other opportunities available, or if your actions at that time were right, even if a situation did not turn out well. Reframing enables you to change the situation in your minds-eye and to incorporate more positive behaviours if you feel yours could have been improved at that time.

If you lost your job because you were continuously late getting into work, you would only have yourself to blame. It's not your boss' fault, it's yours. If you said something in a moment of temper and it changed the dynamics of your connection with that person, you can at least mentally go back and consider how you would deal with a similar situation in the future. You can use reframing to view missed opportunities too and make a mental note of how you will grab the next opportunities with both hands.

So reframing isn't about making you feel bad but allowing you to really learn from your mistakes, or to prepare you for new, exciting opportunities to come. You can't change the past but the great thing is you can learn the lesson and let it shape your future. This is the beneficial part of understanding yourself and looking back.

Looking back and feeling miserable about any mistakes is not conducive to changing your pattern of behaviour. We are all guilty of letting the past envelop us. When something goes badly wrong and you have messed up, you may give yourself a hard time. You may feel guilty, stupid or be consumed with regrets. But, learn from those experiences and develop a new strategy for success. This is the positive approach to failure. Dust yourself off and pick yourself back up.

You don't just learn lessons at school, life is one big learning curve.

Self-Imposed Limitations

When you add self-imposed limitations into the mix, you will tie yourself up into a stranglehold. When life gets so tough that you are scared to make decisions, or you feel a real lack of confidence, you are less likely to be able to achieve your real potential. The best way forward is to develop self-realisation and to make significant changes.

Self-imposed limitations are often tied to your sense of self image and if you have low expectations, well, that's what you will get in life. If you don't believe that you are worth more, then you carve out the reality that you expect. It's easy to follow the lessons learned from your childhood, and using the scenarios that were provided earlier—be unable to stick at a job, not able to stay the course or to have the desire to re-take an exam—but ultimately the message is clear, giving into failure becomes the norm if you don't take a firm stance.

Self-imposed limitations can make you underperform.

Do you ever blame others or the system generally for your lack of success? Do you ever think that you were born unlucky or that someone else has it in for you? True, there will be times when success or failure is not a result of your actions but a direct link to someone else, perhaps losing out at a job interview because another person had more experience than you. Or, perhaps you started up a business and had to watch it fail spectacularly. This type of failure is personal and it hurts, but you can't allow it to affect the future.

You should never buy into that mindset where rich and successful people always believe that they are in control of their destiny. We all have the same free will to make decisions and choices. If you lost an opportunity because you were not successful in a job interview—my question to you would be—how could you develop yourself to being so great and so good at your profession that no one would want to knock you back again? If you can learn to promote yourself and to excel in your chosen field, then you become the person everybody wants. You won't even need to apply for jobs because there will be companies chasing you.

The lesson here is you can't go through life making excuses. Failure comes when you avoid taking risks or start to bypass opportunities that arise, or because you have restricted yourself and set your standards low.

Self-realisation is the key. Because unless you know what you want in life, and have set reasonable standards, how can you achieve much? If your confidence and self-esteem is dragging along the ground, or you are operating on less than healthy pre-conditioned behaviours, you won't be able to move past these confines and success will stay annoyingly out of reach.

If you feel that you have let yourself down, guilt can start to weigh heavily and all those past mistakes or missed opportunities can suddenly start to catch up with you. Do you ever lie in bed at night and wonder why your life has taken such a direction? Do you feel despondent and dread getting up in the morning to go to work? Are you bombarded with regrets that drag you down into the mire?

Although recognition of past failures or any inability to move forward is useful, it's important to free yourself from the guilt, as it will only chain you to the past.

There is no doubt that guilt will impact your self-esteem and drag your confidence down to rock bottom. But, it's worth considering why you are judging yourself and by whose standards are you using?

When you consider your behaviours that may have led you to this point in your life, rather than just give yourself a hard time and compare yourself by someone else's standards, think about the options that were available to you during those times, you may have had few options.

If you had plenty of options, but simply made the wrong choices or took the easy options, then don't judge yourself harshly, learn from those mistakes. Life after all is just one big learning curve, it's time to embrace yours.

Consider the following:

- Why did I act a certain way?
- What were my choices?
- Was I trying to protect myself?
- What did I accomplish overall?

Your actions are likely to be driven by a compulsion to satisfy a need. They help you to:

- Survive
- Protect yourself
- Maintain balance
- Improve/nurture
- Avoid

It's important to ascertain the root of your behaviour. Sure, it may be a learned pattern that is repeated time and time again, but irrespective of this, it's time to take ownership, stand up to the weight of responsibility. Your choices—however well-informed or misinformed—have gotten you to this point, so what are you going to do about it?

Here's how you stop spinning your wheels and break free:

Self-Acceptance

Living self-consciously can be difficult. To be self-accepting doesn't mean accepting that your life will never change, it doesn't mean that you are allowed to lack the desire to improve; rather, it forms the foundations of change. It is more about being conscious of the person you are at this moment in time and to be aware of how you feel so that your route to development is open.

We all have aspects of ourselves that are less pleasing:

- Physical features
- Emotional balance
- Drive
- Jealousy
- Lack of patience, etc.

When you turn your attention inwards and consider the points that you usually try to deny, why not try instead to fully contemplate them? It's important to realise that you are not suddenly going to embrace these aspects of yourself, but this is simply a method of experiencing them without turning to avoidance or denial.

You are as you are now, this is your face, this is your body, and this is your attitude to life. Visualise the person that you are today and do this regularly; gradually you will start to experience fully the tender relationship between your self-esteem and feelings of self-acceptance.

Your life will feel more balanced as a result and importantly, if there are aspects of your being that you feel you must change, you will feel much more motivated to start making those all-important changes but from a place of power. If you cast your mind back to an earlier chapter where I mentioned that the starting point for change must always be with you. Everything that you achieve in life comes down to you; everything that you choose to not do in life comes down to you as well. If a lack of confidence or vision is holding you back, then that's your choice, just know that once you become comfortable and happy with the person you are, holding back can be a thing of the past.

So don't deny any aspect of your being, just instigate those important changes that will benefit you. Always remember you are a blessing and by giving yourself permission that you are worthy of anything you want, it will set you free and release your own inner millionaire.

Here's an example:

Let's imagine you are going to set up a new company, something that means a great deal to you and you are totally focused on achieving success. Perhaps you need to gain financial backing or you need to pitch your business idea to others who can help you progress your dream. Going into any type of meeting can be daunting, especially if there is a lot riding on the outcome. You might feel under pressure, perhaps you're not used to highly pressured situations or this particular meeting has such importance to you personally that you are starting to be governed by the fear of failure. It's important to not fight these feelings but instead to accept them.

Tell yourself "Ok, I am a little scared but that's alright," and then focus on your breathing. When you become nervous, you tense up your whole body, and your breathing becomes shallow, this will only make your voice sound nervous and it will be a higher pitch as a result. But by accepting this emotion and by breathing into it and through it, it will be far easier to control. It may seem difficult initially but once you have highlighted the fear, you can control it and not allow it to define you.

Some successful people have found that they talk to their fears; they ask, "What is the worst that could happen?" This brings those ultimate fears out of the dark and into the light which provides a more balanced reality. These may be deeply-rooted fears, and ones that have had a stranglehold on you for years. If it terrifies you to go into meetings with those high-powered authority figures, or it terrifies you to speak in public, it is worth knowing where these fears have come from. Identify those fears which stop you from moving forward in your life and then determine to get to the root of the fear, as this will reduce the fear or make it disappear altogether. It may free you from the past. These fears are created because you are afraid of making mistakes or of not impressing the person you are about to speak to, and that's because you have placed that person on a pedestal subconsciously; you should never put them on a higher rank than you because it will create a state of intimidation. I'm not saying disregard them, you should respect them, however, believe and know that you are worthy of rubbing your shoulders with great people as well. When you allow yourself to feel this way, nothing will ever intimidate you.

Accepting that fears exist gives you a good starting point. You mustn't feel ashamed by them, we all have fears and many are irrational, but it is how you deal with them that will make a big difference in your life. You don't need to fight your fears, just accept they are real to you and work through them. This way you can disable them. This is the ultimate goal of self-acceptance.

People have a perception that successful or wealthy people don't have fears. Let me make this clear, we all do, the difference is I don't allow fear to paralyse me. I actually use it as inspiration to make sure I conquer it. I remember the first time I was invited to speak on stage to over 5,000 people, let me tell you, I had so much fear inside me before walking onto that stage. However, I chose to focus all my attention on serving the people. I said to myself, "There are 5,000 people who need my help, now go out there and serve them."

It works. Really!

Adjust Your Standards

If you expect next to nothing in life, you are just about guaranteed to achieve next to nothing, it's just the way it is. So, it's important to evaluate your standards and to adjust them accordingly. Don't make the mistake of thinking that you need a job or a business that will enable you to get by in life. Instead think about what you can do to create a career that gives you total financial freedom. If you have the urge to work for yourself, then the sky's the limit. If you open up your mind to see what opportunities exist and to determine if your ideas are valid in the real world, you are stepping into an exciting new life. In fact, you can name your own salary. Isn't that great?

It might seem impossible if your confidence is low, but to evaluate success, look at those who are already successful. How do they think, act and talk differently to you? How high have they set their standards? How do they handle failure when it happens? Use your findings to help raise the bar for your own objectives.

Drop the Deadbeats

We all have friends or associates who seem to spend their lives moaning and groaning about everything. There's always a reason why things go wrong for them and there's always someone else to blame, they might be the nicest people but they are never going to achieve anything. Either they don't realise how they are behaving or they don't want to change and that's fine. These are the deadbeat type of people that you may have gravitated towards during those times when life was tough and your confidence was rock bottom. Dropping the deadbeat doesn't mean never talking or associating with them again, but it's about daring to set your standards higher and to embrace other more successful people in your life too.

What's wrong with becoming friendly with those who have a more positive frame of mind? Do you hold back from doing this because you're worried that they may be better than you? Do you dislike change and worry about meeting new people? Do you feel it is better to stick to the people you know? Maybe some of your friends have told you that you have changed? Sticking close to your local circle is often not about loyalty but comes down to fear again. New social circles equate to your being a small fish in a large pond rather than being the big fish in a small pond.

It makes sense to surround yourself with positive energy and with others who achieve. It's not copying, it's about developing their instincts for success.

Think about successful people, do they:

- Have more creativity?
- Work harder?
- Have more dedication?
- Create luck?
- Have a get up and go attitude?
- Seize new opportunities?
- Have more drive?
- Have a big why?
- Have a purpose?
- Have a big vision?
- Have an open-mind?

Don't plateau by hanging around with those who will never overtake you, because where's the motivation to succeed? Instead surround yourself with those who seem to be doing better than you and determine to emulate their mindset, embrace challenges instead of ducking them, work harder, and strive towards positive goals. That's a good thing—right?

Become an observer. Watch those people around you; watch what they do that is different to you. Sometimes it's the smallest things than that can make the biggest difference. It isn't about copying others; it's about questioning the way you think and the way that you do things currently and about embracing more positive values in life.

What's holding you back?

- Preconditioned behaviours?
- Low self-esteem?
- Low expectations?
- Negative attitude?

- Fear of failure?
- Self limitations?

Steve Jobs Case Study

Steve Jobs should be a great example for you to never give up on your dreams and aspirations; he was someone who oozed those inner millionaire traits that eventually made him achieve billionaire status.

Steve dropped out of college after six months and spent the next 18 months dropping in on creative classes, including a course on calligraphy. In the commencement address he gave at Stanford, Jobs said that, while he continued to audit classes at Reed, he slept on the floor in friends' dorm rooms, returned Coke bottles for food money, and got weekly free meals at the local Hare Krishna temple. In that same speech, Jobs said: "If I had never dropped in on that single calligraphy course in college, the Mac would have never had multiple typefaces or proportionally spaced fonts" (Wikipedia reference).

Steve was a man with a global vision; he had the belief within himself that he would do whatever it takes. The inner millionaire will not let pride be their demise; it will not paralyse them in the pursuit of their goals.

Steve Jobs slept on the floor and sold coke bottles in order to eat. There are so many more people like Steve, such as American Billionaire Mark Cuban who ate mustard and ketchup sandwiches, and slept on the floor of a 3 bedroom apartment that housed him and 5 buddies. Both these guys came from humble beginnings.

Mr Jobs was a college dropout. Can you imagine how many people told him he was stupid to give up on his education? One of things about the inner millionaire it will not allow the opinion of others get in their way.

In 1976, Steve Wozniak single-handedly invented the Apple Computer I. After Wozniak showed it to Jobs, who suggested that they sell it, they formed Apple Computers, along with Ronald Wayne, in the garage of Steve Job's parents, in order to sell it. Wayne stayed only a short time, leaving Jobs and Wozniak as the primary co-founders of the company. They received funding from a then semi-retired Intel product marketing manager and engineer, Mike Markkula. Scott McNealy, one of the co-founders of Sun Microsystems, said that Jobs broke a "glass age ceiling" in Silicon Valley because he'd created a very successful company at a young age.

In 1978, Apple recruited Mike Scott from National Semiconductor to serve as CEO for what turned out to be several turbulent years. In 1983, Jobs lured John Sculley away from Pepsi-Cola to serve as Apple's CEO, asking, "Do you want to spend the rest of your life selling sugared water, or do you want a chance to change the world?" (Wikipedia reference).

Wow! What a question.

Steve demonstrated a service to the world in that statement. *The Inner Millionaire* is about providing value to the world, it's about creating something bigger than money. Steve's focus was not about making millions or billions of dollars, he was focused on contributing to the world and the money was a result of that ideology.

Bill Gates' vision was also having a computer in every household around the world. This is a massive lesson for everybody when your purpose is bigger than your individual needs, and that's when empires and wealth is created.

Take a great look at your life right now, look at your business and ask yourself, is your purpose bigger than your individual needs?

In the early 1980s, Jobs was among the first to see the commercial potential of Xerox PARC's mouse-driven graphical user interface, which led to the creation of the Apple Lisa. A year later, Apple completed the Macintosh.

The following year, Apple aired a Super Bowl television commercial titled "1984". At Apple's annual shareholders meeting on January 24, 1984, a very emotional Jobs introduced the Macintosh to a wildly enthusiastic audience; Andy Hertzfeld described the scene as "pandemonium".

While Jobs was a persuasive and charismatic director for Apple, some of his employees from that time described him as an erratic and temperamental manager. Disappointing sales caused deterioration in Jobs's working relationship with Sculley, which devolved into a power struggle between the two. Jobs kept meetings running past midnight, sent out lengthy faxes, and then called new meetings at 7:00 a.m.

During an April 10 and 11 board meeting, Apple's board of directors gave Sculley the authority to remove Jobs from all roles, except as chairman, to reassign him to an undetermined position. John delayed a reassignment. But when Sculley learned that Jobs—who believed Sculley to be "bad for Apple" and the wrong person to lead the company—had been attempting to organise a boardroom coup, on May 24, 1985, he called a board meeting to resolve the matter. Apple's board of directors sided with Sculley once again and removed Jobs from his managerial duties as head of the Macintosh division. With no duties, and exiled from the rest of the company to an otherwise-empty building, Jobs stopped coming to work and later resigned as chairman. After unsuccessfully applying to fly on the Space Shuttle as a civilian astronaut, and briefly considering starting a computer company in the Soviet Union, he resigned from Apple five months later (Wikipedia reference).

Does this surprise you that even a billionaire fails?

Well it shouldn't because, as mentioned previously, everybody has failed, from the richest person in the world to the most challenged people. Failure is a part of life. We must accept it and embrace it.

Next time you experience failure or a setback, ask yourself how Steve Jobs might deal with the same situation.

In a speech Jobs gave at Stanford University in 2005, he said being fired from Apple was the best thing that could have happened to him; "The heaviness of being successful was replaced by the lightness of being a beginner again, less sure about everything. It freed me to enter one of the most creative periods of my life." And he added, "I'm pretty sure none of this would have happened if I hadn't been fired from Apple. It was awful-tasting medicine, but I guess the patient needed it."(Wikipedia reference).

Steve Jobs is the example of how to respond to failure; this is a guy who was sacked by his own team, the company that he created from nothing, all taken away from him within a seconds.

How would you feel if this happened to you? How would you respond?

I can tell you most people would fall into depression, quit and do nothing. They would share the story of betrayal to the people around them. In most people eyes this would be the end of their dream. However not for Steve Jobs—the inner millionaire was still alive and well he kept on persevering.

During some ups and downs in 2003 and 2004, as Pixar's contract with Disney was running out, Jobs and Disney chief executive Michael Eisner tried but failed to negotiate a new partnership, and in early 2004, Jobs announced that Pixar would seek a new partner to distribute its films after its contract with Disney expired.

In October 2005, Bob Iger replaced Eisner at Disney, and Iger quickly worked to mend relations with Jobs and Pixar. On January 24, 2006, Jobs and Iger announced that Disney had agreed to purchase Pixar in an all-stock transaction worth $7.4 billion. When the deal closed, Jobs became The Walt Disney Company's largest single shareholder with approximately seven percent of the company's stock. Jobs's holdings in Disney far exceeded those of Eisner, who held 1.7 percent, and of Disney family member Roy E. Disney, who until his 2009 death held about one percent of the company's stock and whose criticisms of Eisner—especially that he soured Disney's relationship with Pixar—accelerated Eisner's ousting. Upon completion of the merger, Jobs received 7% of Disney shares, and joined the Board of Directors as the largest individual shareholder.

In 1996, Apple announced that it would buy NeXT for $427 million. The deal was finalised in February 1997, bringing Jobs back to the company he co-founded (Wikipedia reference).

Steve Jobs is a role model to the world, he is the symbol of a warrior who kept on fighting and used failure as an inspiration. He never stopped believing in his vision and now has created a worldwide legacy and his name will always be remembered. This is the inner millionaire speaking to you, in actual fact, in his honour, it's the inner billionaire.

Introducing Self-Sabotage

When looking at how to incorporate positive changes, it's impossible to avoid discussing self-sabotage because it's such a common occurrence. You may have heard of the expression but it's possible you are guilty of it without realising. It is a destructive force that serves to undermine the positive or appropriate course of action and instead only violates your goals and values. The key to the inner millionaire is to stop yourself from sabotaging your chances in life and start to recognise the behaviour and to understand why.

Learning more about you the person, understanding what makes you tick, may be a painful journey down memory lane, but it's a healthy thing to do because it shows that you want to improve your life and to become successful. It's about peeling back the layers that make up your personality, shredding those layers that are doing you more harm than good and inserting new healthy layers that make up for a better way of life.

Think of the self saboteur aspect as a naughty child that lives within, because self sabotage requires you to often act in a less than adult way and is reminiscent of those childish actions. When you grow into adulthood, and if your examples in life have been fair, honest and balanced to-date, you're able to deal with most things, from emotional issues, relationships to your career and financial prospects. You have a well-rounded attitude towards the end goal. But when your examples in life have been far from balanced, it's likely that the self-saboteur will emerge more regularly.

Simply understand that your adult self is really the boss, you make the decisions, you should be wise enough to act with common sense, you should be rational and able to face all the world can throw at you. When you are faced with very difficult scenarios, your very naughty, childlike saboteur can start to act like a tyrant, undermining that desired common sense approach, it can push you to act irrationally. You start to act not on facts but on fears, possibly damaging yourself and your prospects in the process.

It may sound ridiculous, but it happens more times than you might be aware.

If you have been an argument with a partner, a colleague or even with your boss, you may find that you have said things in an outburst to taunt and provoke, knowing that the resulting actions were going to hurt you but, irrespective of the outcome, your need to do so outweighed the risks.

Learning How to Rein In That Saboteur is All-Important

We all want to feel loved, appreciated, nurtured, satisfied and secure and we want to have confirmation of just how great we are, but there is a need to feel respected and to be praised when we have done a good job too. We want to feel valued.

Your inner child requires others to satisfy this need and in doing so, this confirms your sense of value. But if you are a self-confident and well-balanced individual, you will not need the compliments or verification from others because already you know who you are and what you have to do to achieve. When you lack self-esteem, are bound by limitations, or have pre-conditioned ideas, the self-saboteur may rise to the surface more times than is healthy.

Here's an example:

If you were constantly criticised in your younger years, it's quite easy to see how self-sabotage would become a part of everyday life. Being criticised is a negative action and it wounds. It can impact self-esteem and confidence and make you have less faith in your own abilities going forward. When you're in that situation, whether it is your parents, your siblings, your teachers or any of your friends, it undermines your belief to be able to achieve. In other words, it rocks your foundations to the core.

It will make you strive all the more to be complemented, to be admired, and to be praised. You will need this public endorsement of who you are. So instead of seeking out ways to become successful in your own right, the hard work goes into pleasing others. You choose the wrong end game. This can carry on into your adult life meaning that you can only feel good about yourself when you are recognised by others.

Can you see how this is not a healthy behaviour?

Of course it's great to have a boss tell you that you have done a great job, it can give you a real buzz to know that your hard work has paid off and your work is recognised, If you are self-employed and you have just finished a project for a client and they tell you that they love the work you have done, this will affirm your talent and you will feel great. But for some people, there is an intrinsic need to have verbal confirmation of their abilities all of the time and this is often a pre-conditioned behaviour.

But what happens if an employer makes you feel bad about the level of work you do? Some bosses take great delight in keeping their staff in place, ruling by fear and making them too scared to progress. Derogatory remarks can really wound. It's all too easy to feel despondent and to let it chip away at your self-esteem. The solution is to have awareness and realisation that you are worth more. No one should have the power over you to make you feel bad, but if your confidence is low already and your pre-learned behaviours are telling you that this is acceptable, you need to consider why, identify where these beliefs have come from and to change your perspective on the work front. There's a big world out there and if you develop some entrepreneurial spirit, you could be running your own empire instead.

Self-sabotage can occur through a number of instances or triggers, but if you are recognising aspects of your own personality here, they no doubt come from feelings of insecurity, guilt, self-hatred, self-doubt, and through fear.

If you are reading this and thinking "No way, I like being me" that's great and you should, providing, you really, really mean that. There is a big difference between standing up and saying that you are happy in yourself and you like the way you are and actually believing it.

Have you ever been told:

- Your work is poor?
- You've failed?
- You're not good enough?
- You're not lovable?

Well guess what?

You are not the only one and you won't be the last. Your inner millionaire will not allow the poison of others to choke you into a world of darkness; there have been many greats who were ridiculed and told they were not good enough.

When Winston Churchill was a young man, his father concluded that Winston was unfit for a career in law or politics because he did so badly in school.

While studying in Dublin, Churchill was rarely visited by his mother, and wrote letters begging her either to come to the school or to allow him to come home. His relationship with his father was distant; he once remarked that they barely spoke to one another.

This is the relationship of many children growing up and so many parents will apply pressure and stress on their kids to live a life that they want, not for the best interest of the child wants. So many people feel that they need to get the approval of their parents or want to hear the words "I'm proud of you" or "I believe in you" and never get it.

These kind of thoughtless comments occur often and even if the intention is not to hurt or to demoralise your confidence, it doesn't take much to fracture the basic foundations of esteem and to leave you acting in ways to prove that you are good while deep inside you don't really believe it.

If this sounds like you, then remember Winston Churchill became a British politician who was the Prime Minister of the United Kingdom from 1940 to 1945 and again from 1951 to 1955. Widely regarded as one of the greatest wartime leaders of the 20th century, Churchill was also an officer in the British Army, a historian, a writer (as Winston S. Churchill), and an artist. Churchill is the only British Prime Minister to have won the Nobel Prize in Literature since its inception in 1901, and was the first person to be made an honorary citizen of the United States (Wikipedia reference).

Winston was like any other child seeking the love of his parents and he didn't do well at school.

I hear so many people always ask, why me? This occurs when things don't go their way.

What people forget is, it's not about, "Why me?" Because it's also happening to everybody else but sometimes we forget due to being trapped into our own world.

People will criticise you or make fun of your ideas or even actively try to stop you. However we have to understand that in most situations their efforts to stop you are only attempts to protect you from failure.

Please remember that failure will only happen *if you stop*. If you keep going, a "failure" is just another learning experience. And besides, giving up on a heartfelt aspiration is worse than failing. "Many people die," said Oliver Wendell Holmes, "with their music still in them." That's true tragedy.

So allow your inner millionaire to shine.

Overcoming That Self-Saboteur

So now that you've probably dug a little deeper into your personal life than you expected and you may be feeling a little raw and exposed, but the good news is that you can quieten that self-saboteur and overcome all this negative stuff. It just takes a willingness to say, "Yep that's me and I don't want to be like this anymore." Take responsibility and control how you act and think.

It's important to stop judging yourself but to live life to the full and go for it.

So, here's how you make positive changes:

Consider all of the ways that you have self-sabotaged yourself— whether personally or professionally. Really think hard about this and write down notes, once you start you may be surprised at how much comes out. But that's okay.

Now consider why you have acted in these ways. What drives you to self-destruct or to underachieve?

Ask yourself open ended questions so that you have to deliver an answer such as, "What am I hoping to achieve by not starting my business?" Or, "why am I not applying for big, well-paid roles?"

Start your questions with who, what, why, where or when and this will make you have to consider your answer.

If you've been honest with your questions and answers, you may discover that you've unearthed some startling revelations about yourself and from this point, you can now establish what you don't want to tolerate in life. You can also establish what is important to you and how you progress going forward. This then goes back to the goal setting stage, not just in terms of finances and a career, but those core values which provide the foundations in a personal sense so that you are able to achieve success.

Examine Your Belief System

You will now have discovered that not everything you will have been told, or have been taught in life is correct. But you are a smart individual and you can make up your own mind as to what is right and wrong. You can banish negative thoughts and self-doubts and instead, you can do all the things that make a positive impact on your life.

Your core beliefs are pretty important because they are responsible for your ability to gain financial well-being or get stuck in the quagmire of poverty. They can generate wonderful relationships or terrible ones; they can give you happiness in life or great deal of misery.

But you are not stuck with your beliefs.

It's always a good idea to examine your core beliefs and then to keep them in mind while you consider which areas of your life needs to be addressed. Let's assume you're not happy in your existing work role and you always feel overlooked within the company, feel dissatisfied, undervalued, less liked than you would want to be and you feel stressed. You may even currently blame your boss, your colleagues or the role for your lack of success, but maybe, just maybe, your beliefs are tainted by past perceptions. The inner millionaire will never come up with excuses and try to blame external factors but will take ownership of their results.

Ask yourself:

- Did you choose the job?
- Did you make the decision to stay?
- Could you apply for different roles within the company or externally?
- Do you moan about being overlooked or have you just self-sabotaged your potential for more?
- If you really hate what you are doing, why are you not looking at ways to create your own ventures in life?

Just remember that your truth will change as you become more informed and achieve a much greater level of understanding. So, with each obstacle you overcome, you gain wisdom. Our system in life doesn't teach individuals to really understand who they are or what their potential is. It doesn't teach people how to face up to reality, how to overcome difficulties and do it with a smile. The system labels you before you have even had a chance to reach your potential. It may be wrong but that is our society. But you don't have to be pigeon-holed. You can break free from the labels or from your understanding of the world. As long as you strive for more, it is there.

Self-Image is Created Out of Your Beliefs

Your beliefs are also the fundamental building blocks to a successful you, so you can see how important they are. Your learned behaviours form your beliefs, new experiences can alter or confirm those beliefs, your memories, your observations also add to those beliefs. You may feel a good or bad person, or a successful or unsuccessful person because of these beliefs.

You may feel worthless or you may feel amazing because of your beliefs.

Ask yourself:

- Do you take risks in life?
- Do you yearn to learn new things?
- Do you consider yourself brave?
- Do you embrace change?

If not, consider why not and which beliefs may be limiting your potential. You may or may not like the person that you are today, you may or may not like the way your life is going today, you may feel unsatisfied that you have not achieved in life, but today, you can embed healthy new messages within that will enable you to start changing all your tomorrows because the inner millionaire lives within you.

The Real Reason People Fear Failure

The reason why most people have a fear of failure during their working careers is because of those impressionable childhood years. Yes, it means going all the way back to those tender years and checking out those early conditioned behaviours because the chances are your fears started there. If you are nervous to strive forward in your life, you may have been programmed that failure is a bad thing and that you should avoid risk. If so, no wonder you are afraid to go all out for your goals.

When we were children at school and we received an F in our exams or assignments, in most cases, it was a humiliating and embarrassing experience, so as children we attached a painful, disempowering meaning such as, "this is too hard, I'm not smart enough" or "I can't do this" and as we experienced more failures, we would attach additional pain that continues disempowering us.

We were not taught that failure is simply feedback or how to ask the right questions like, what can I learn from this?

The most successful and wealthiest people in the world have failed many times; however, the inner millionaire will not allow failure to paralyse them, and in actual fact, it empowers them to continue until they achieve the goal intended.

The problem is this, in society we label things, we label fail and pass, fail is, "You are not good enough" and pass is, "You are smart, well done." What people need to understand is that one of the key ingredients to wealth and success is failure. It's true, in order to succeed, you will fail.

Chapter 6

The Life Skills Everybody Should Develop

Schools could have certainly taken the responsibility for an introduction into the inner millionaire mindset. Practical skills would enable us to grow into confident, emotionally sound, and life-savvy individuals. This could include:

- How to negotiate
- Teaching kids how to be creative
- The importance of providing value
- How to deal with conflict
- How to manage money
- The importance of creating more than one income

Starting this type of learning process from a young age can only help to embed the importance of each student needing to grasp these life skills. When the information forms a natural part of the syllabus, and learning is fun, they should learn readily, absorbing these skills quickly providing an understanding for the rest of their lives. Practical skills should sit alongside the need to read and write.

But we know that this just does not happen. As teenagers we were thrust into the world of adulthood, barely prepared for the stresses and requirements of real life. It's a big shock for many.

Throughout this book I have expressed the importance of each person being able to feel confident, to be able to shrug off negative ways, to relearn positive behaviours and to seize the moment if they wish to lead a successful life, so doesn't it make sense that we teach people how to embrace their full potential and unleash the inner millionaire mindset from an early age? It doesn't matter what age you are when you determine to change your life, if you are focussed on change, you can do anything. But, it is certainly easier to grasp opportunities with both hands when younger and this is why we should be teaching children how to overcome obstacles, how to jump back up when faced with failure and how to dream about the potentials of life.

Look back at your own informative years. Did you enjoy school? Was it a positive time in your life? Have you, like so many other people, realised just how easy school was compared to the real world? Imagine how you might feel today if you could have learned a much wider range of knowledge and skills that the inner millionaire possesses.

Do you think you would be:

- More confident?
- More successful?
- More prepared to take risks?
- Less afraid of failure?

This book isn't about ripping apart the failings of the school curriculum, it is about determining ways that can make everyone reach their full potential, even if that means looking back at the foundations of your life to see how a different approach and an altered way of thinking could have made things a whole lot different for you today.

I often think about my own childhood. It was a happy one in many ways, certainly in comparison with others, but, I would have loved to have been encouraged during my early entrepreneurial years and to not feel as if a door was slammed shut on all of my ideas by everyone— metaphorically speaking. Instinctively, I knew that I wanted to set up in a business and to have some of my ideas help me make it to the big time, but when you are told, time and time again, that your ideas are just not going to work in the real world, it's deeply disappointing and it strips away the desire to keep pushing through feelings of rejection.

This isn't a slight on my parents, most parents do the best job that they can in some difficult situations, but some children don't want to fit into the traditional ways of learning, progressing through school and then emerging to spend time scrambling about looking for a job which might pay well but is miserably boring. They need to invent, they need to explore, and they need to think big.

Being a parent is one of the toughest jobs ever, but even with the best will in the world, it can be a struggle for them to find time in a manic day to ensure that they encourage, rather than squash, the future potential of their offspring through falling into the trap of their own learned behaviours.

This is easier said than done of course because to recognise the need to change means that they have to take time to scrutinise their own upbringings. This takes a lot of self-development and a willingness to embark upon a journey of change.

Equally, some adults may just not be able to impart the skills in an informative and patient way, so it would of made sense that schools take up the mantle? As adults, we know it's easy to make costly mistakes in life and although many students cannot wait to embrace adult life, the reality will be vastly different than the fantasy.

Working for a living is hard work. Going into a job that is dull and low paid is not living the dream or embracing the inner millionaire way. Suddenly, life becomes a lot more demanding than it was in school. In an ideal world, when we left school it would been brilliant to be fully-equipped to cope with all problems. We would know the fundamentals of how to succeed in life, learning how to overcome the inevitable knock-backs, how to manage our time, how to develop good relationships with others outside of our typical circle of friends and to live the dream.

But it's true to say that some have very little idea of how to get by in real life.

Consider your own teenage years and that joyous moment of leaving school for good. Looking back, do you feel that you were totally prepared?

There is no doubt that schools today teach many valuable skills but individuals have to learn all skills—financial responsibilities, for one. Unfortunately, when we leave school, we often have no idea about money and so we enter into a world where easy cash is readily available and banks, keen to snaffle up those school leavers with good credit, offer credit cards to those who have jobs. But there is often a temptation to overspend and it is easy to see how teenagers start to develop bad financial habits.

Required Skills

But it's not all about the financial implications either, even though knowing how to create new revenue streams and to manage money is incredibly important. The inner millionaire develops amazing communication skills, conversation is vitally important because it really permeates every aspect of life today as we know it. Individuals must know how to express themselves and to make themselves understood. This includes verbal conversations, either face-to-face or over the telephone, and written communications, such as letters, e-mails, and social media. The trend today is to use social media outlets to communicate and this often requires shortened or abbreviated messages, resulting in poor spelling and also reduced face-to-face communications.

There are many positives to living in the modern world, with technology being so far advanced. Many opportunities are created as a result but the downside is that there can be social isolation and a lack of development with social skills because there is a natural barrier when people stop interacting in the same way. Text speak has crucified the English language and many adults are now seemingly unable to string an intelligent sentence together.

The school environment successfully (in the main) teaches children how to interact with others. This is good networking practice and something that should be continued right through life. Unless you are a social media enthusiast or find that within your business you have to network with others, communicating, and building rapport, creates strong bonds that naturally lead to successful encounters. Some people can find themselves struggling to adapt otherwise and to forge strong relationships. We take friendships for granted during the school years but often on leaving school, life starts to present a wide range of other opportunities, this means losing touch with many friends. Many people are now struggling with these natural skills because they were not utilised or endorsed enough when growing up.

If you have children, you may have slipped into the financial trap that your own parents did. It does seem to follow suit through the generations and again, points the finger towards learned behaviours being so important, i.e. negative behaviours needing to be changed while positive behaviours should remain.

Following on from this, you may have had many dreams and aspirations as a child, but did you envisage you would be where you are today? It's always a good idea to reflect on your journey but to do so in a positive way, for example:

- If you had taken a different path, what would you be doing now?
- Would this have been better for you?
- What stopped you?
- Is it too late to change the outcome?

Many parents work in dead end jobs just so they can pay the bills, but the last thing that they will want is for their children to end up in the same way. But if adults struggle to clamber out of the quagmire of life, how can they teach their children the importance of having dreams and about striving for success and making money, if they can't do it themselves?

Because life can be just a struggle (unless you have learned how to fulfil your ambitions and to reach the dizzy heights of success) most parents do not advocate stepping off the straight and narrow of learning and will want their offspring to follow the same route into the career years in the most proficient way possible.

As such, you can bet that most parents would not recommend their children to start up their own businesses or to dream big. They will be too worried about the day-to-day stuff. It's a case of reeling their children's ideas back in and teaching them that working hard and being loyal to an employer counts.

You can understand why this happens, even if encouraging children to follow their dreams while applying a practical application towards those goals would be much more rewarding.

The Power of Thought

We all think, thinking is natural and instinctive isn't it?

But being able to apply logic and to be able to think clearly and effectively is high up on the list of must-have skills. The inner millionaire is about individuals who can think for themselves, can problem-solve, make decisions, and have the ability to succeed in life. Some decisions are not easy ones to make and therefore making the wrong ones can have huge consequences. The inner millionaire will always analyse any situation so that snap decisions are avoided. It's important, not just for the individual's sake but for others around them.

Nothing is black-and-white and certain situations need more clarity. This enables the individual to suss out all of the implications. Education does little to test the ability of young adults, the old style of teaching can also hinder people's ability to grasp reasoning, they may be taught to listen and to make notes but not necessarily how to think through and to solve a problem through to solution. Much is memorised instead which will not help the individual later on. The art of debating is always useful but not used in every school. Many parents also teach their kids not to ask many questions because it's rude, so people grow without knowing how to ask the right questions.

Practical Skills

During school, some practical skills are learned, such as home economics, i.e. cooking and sewing, and then there are the inevitable woodworking and metalwork skills but more should be done in schools to teach us essential life skills. Here's an example:

We have to buy something for 50 cents and then have to consider how to sell it to somebody else for $1. These kinds of exercises would create a very strong entrepreneurial foundation and ignite the inner millionaire attitude. Some theory coupled with practical assignments can enable these individuals to be prepared for tasks that are likely to happen later on.

Car maintenance is another skill likely to be needed, although it would be impossible to cover every mechanical eventuality, learning how to change a tyre, or to add oil or water would be useful. So by teaching your kids these skills, you can also give them a life lesson on the exchange of goods and services, meaning when your child comes to you because they want you to buy something for them, you can barter with them by telling them to change the oil and check the water and tyre pressure of the car and then they will get what they want. This also encourages healthy negotiation skills.

The Financials

It is easy to see how important it is to be able to handle money in a responsible fashion. People have to learn a successful money management system and those who are rich and wealthy will have a method or strategy on how they distribute their money and this is something that I teach in my program. For those who really want to go into business for themselves, having knowledge of how to set-up the structure of their new company, tax information, cash flow and how to reinvest into the company is crucial.

What is the world today without having good credit? The answer is tough. Everybody starts with a clean slate, i.e. they have no credit at all and so the banks are very happy to dish out their first credit cards, which of course help to gain credit worthiness, although this can quickly backfire. This is unless people generally understand the importance of being credit worthy. The inner millionaire understands that plastic money can be a very tempting option. However they will understand the difference between good debt and bad debt.

The problem for those emerging into the work force is that credit cards will not seem like money to them, but it hurts them when the payments have to be made back. With good education, a better relationship with money could be established ensuring that those new credit ratings don't take an early dent. Understanding the implications of paying bills later than the due date or only paying the minimal payments could help all to develop good financial acumen and to avoid getting into bad debt.

Employment

When we went to school, knowledge provided its own rewards, but part of schools' goals nowadays should be to prepare those kids to find a job and to enable them to excel within their chosen careers. It's about preparing them so that they contribute in society and so they are productive and self-sufficient, in other words, they are well-rounded individuals. So finding a job is absolutely crucial, but, as previously stated, there are other options. It's not all about joining the rat race. It's about going after your dreams but doing so in a prepared manner.

We all have to fend for ourselves and to be able to earn enough money to be able to fulfil life's ambitions. Embracing an inner millionaire mindset would help schools prepare those students newly emerging into society to know how to get what they want. These individuals will conquer and face the terrifying interview stage; to be confident during this process would enable all to gain better employment, but it's not just about the job interview stage, it's about how to create a C.V.

It's also about how to apply for work, how to write a good cover letter, or to review employment contracts if a job offer is made.

But, again, for those who apply the inner millionaire way, they may wish to get a business loan and to set up their own business, so knowing how to prepare the documentation to secure financial backing could be the big difference between the business happening or failing at the first hurdle. For the entrepreneur, this type of information is invaluable.

Some people are naturally good at communicating and presenting themselves in a professional manner and so it is likely that some of the best opportunities will go to those people, so the majority of people would benefit from understanding the whole employment ethos, how do they make an impact within the workforce? Have they improved their chances of getting the job? What sort of job should they go for? Do they have the relevant skill-sets? Do they need to go onto college to enable them to get a chance of having their desired future?

I believe our schools could educate school leavers to a much higher level and include practical skills so that they are one step nearer to approaching adulthood in a more confident manner.

Currently, schools provide the opportunity for students to get out there in the real world and to try out some work experience paces, but it could be useful to extend these placements:

- One week in an office environment—how to structure your day in business.
- One week in retail—learn how to communicate and sell
- One week in a community environment—learning how to work in a team environment.
- One week at a hospital—experience a sense of gratitude, etc.

This would enable students to understand what life is all about and to fuel their desire to go into the marketplace as enthusiastic and as prepared as possible, which will start to engage their inner millionaire skill-sets.

Failing

No one wants to fail in life but if we do not learn how to cope with failure or rejection, it will really impact our confidence levels and is something we should have learned before leaving school. It is all very well protecting individuals during the school system or in life, but life isn't fair sometimes and learning how to overcome knock-backs is actually a good lesson to learn.

Dealing with failure is tough, so being able to tap into our inner millionaire to develop clarity of thought will enable each person to be able to analyse the situation fully. People need to be able to recognise options that are available to them so that they can find a route towards success. People often fear taking risks, because the competitiveness in challenging oneself at work, at school sports or to compete academically has now been greatly reduced. Subsequently and unsurprisingly, these individuals won't know what has hit them if they fail at getting their dream job, or if they get made redundant.

Rejection and failure is a part of life and missing out on a potential promotion is not unrealistic. It can dent that individual's self-esteem and lower their confidence levels substantially. However when you have programmed the inner millionaire mindset to be active within, you will know how to respond in those situations just like some of the greats. Failure will provide positive outcomes, however it means that the individual needs to look at their current ways of doing things and to reinvent them, with the view that they will achieve success through doing so. Failure and learning to fight back comes from that inspired objective which will allow the individual to be tougher, to be more resilient and to have greater character. Learning how to overcome all odds is a fantastic toolset to have.

Time Management

To be successful, you have to know how to manage your time effectively. So much time gets wasted when simply having the ability to streamline processes can make a huge difference to the success rate of an individual and to any company. The skill of time management is the foundation of success knowing where to spend your energy to optimise maximise results. The inner millionaire mindset is organised so they will adhere to deadlines. It's important for adults to be able to stick to schedules and to be able to juggle any work expectations. Learning these skills will enable the individual to avoid taking on too much pressure and experiencing feelings of inadequacy.

Learning to Fail

I believe the global education system could certainly do more to improve people's real-life learning, providing them with practical skills that would improve their ability to manage their life. Unfortunately the education system doesn't concentrate on the day-to-day skills needed; it would appear that schools set the students up to fail, rather than assuring them of a confident rite of passage.

The problem is that during childhood, we were mainly taught to memorise the information given. Of course, to a certain degree this has to be the case because there is a great deal of knowledge that has to be imparted to us if we were going to be able to pass our exams, but learning parrot fashion is not conducive to learning those critical life skills.

Historically, the onus has always been on parents' taking responsibility for teaching their children the more practical skills that are required in life, but when you consider that parents aren't always qualified themselves to teach these types of lessons, it makes sense that the school environment would have been the perfect place to learn.

Currently, schools lack the type of training material that would be highly useful in the real world; information such as emotional intelligence training, good communication skills, financial planning and personal development would make a big difference to current school leavers and in fact to adults generally.

With these small adjustments to the school curriculum, it would make sense to incorporate some of the skills into classes that already exist. If you think about the maths class, once the basics have been taught and understood, why not talk about credit ratings, interest rates and the financial implications of not being able to manage money?

English classes could also focus on debating and communication so at least some of the skills are being covered. There could also be after-school classes which would teach other essential life skills.

When you consider that life is all about making very important decisions about the future starting from the tender age of 13, it makes sense to apply the inner millionaire attitude which would help all to make better decisions.

Self-Promotion

We are taught to be modest and to not be cocky, but having an inner confidence and high self-esteem certainly helps in life. Selling is often tagged as taboo. Who likes someone who brags or who thinks they know it all? But actually, being confident and having the skills to sell your abilities in life will make you a great attribute for any business venture, but especially for your own.

If you consider successful entrepreneurs like Richard Branson or Warren Buffet, they don't just sell themselves, they sell a culture. Having strong, solid skills and a drive to succeed are all that you need in life. Don't worry about making mistakes, only worry about not learning from them. Many of the top businesses today have floundered or failed in the early days. Remove the tag of selling yourself of being wrong, and concentrate on your strengths in life.

It's important for you to realise that there is a whole world of opportunity out there irrespective of experiences, qualifications or skills. The more informed you are, the easier the route towards success but knowing that you have the strength to overcome tough times and to work through times of failure is going to help.

Deciding on a career is daunting of course. Starting up a business can be a terrifying prospect too but it also opens up a great many opportunities. Knowing what is needed to succeed in any venture will certainly make things easier, but sometimes it's just a giant leap into the unknown, fuelled by excitement and certainty and backed by the knowledge of how it all needs to be set up.

Great coaches will guide you and mentor you, more so if you want to set up in business. It may seem to be a risky challenge to the average person setting up a business, but actually the financial markets and job opportunities are always likely to be unstable. The economy should never be a reason to stop people chasing after their dreams and realising that they can have anything they want in life, providing they go after it.

The inner millionaire is alive and kicking inside everyone, but most people don't set the green light to go, because they have an unhealthy association with money, they self-sabotage or have deeply rooted limitations that will just hold them back anyway. It's hard to instil in everyone that they have the potential to achieve all that they want because most people are held back by what they think they deserve, and that's a very different scenario altogether.

If only the system would teach people to make the most of their opportunities or to create them, they could approach working life with zest and creativity and the rewards could be far greater. If we stopped labelling people and started to encourage those around us, think of the potential achievements. Sadly, society frowns upon success stories in many ways, but don't let that stop you from reaching for the stars, you have the ability to achieve all of your goals and it doesn't matter how hard the journey is to get there. The end result will always be more satisfying.

Making Changes

There will be those forward thinking young adults who have the capacity to be adventurous and successful in an entrepreneurial way, think of:

Ben Way – who started his first business at the age of 15 and was worth £25 million in his teens.

Ben Cohen – who started his business at the age of 16 and who became a millionaire.

Mark Zuckerberg – who co-founded Facebook from his dorm room and is now a billionaire.

These are just three examples of individuals who have made their names and created great wealth from an early age. We should always be encouraging those with ideas to break free of the limitations that are placed upon them, not just through themselves but the limitations imposed by society in general. You don't need to have wealth or life experiences to generate great ideas.

Can you imagine someone telling Mark Zuckerberg that no one would be interested in messing about on Facebook? It's a good thing that some entrepreneurs determine to do it anyway.

The current ethos in those great halls of learning is to promote a traditional employment route starting from those exam options and following on to the moment when the individual leaves school. It is true that currently those leaving school may be misinformed or even ill-prepared but they know that they have to get out there and to start working for a living, even if it is a job that they don't like, because that's what happens in life.

But it doesn't need to.

So many people end up in careers that they dislike intently but it's never too late to change a route in life. If we take a look at Belinda who had her heart set on becoming a nutritionist. Unlike many of her age, she was not put off by the years of required study.

She went to college and passed all of the exams, moving onto university. Belinda was still studying diligently in her early 20s. It became apparent at university that she no longer found her chosen career as exciting or as satisfying as she had imagined.

Belinda was lucky; she had a supportive family background and parents who recognised the need for her to change her career. Because she had thought long and hard about her options, and by this time had a great deal of experience as a young adult, she realised that her career path was going to be vastly different than she had initially expected. Although daunting, she was prepared to continue with her studies. Belinda went into Law which meant going back to college to get additional qualifications before moving onto university where she finally qualified and was ready to emerge into the workplace at the age of 29.

The point here is that Belinda had the courage to stand up and say she had made a mistake. In financial terms it was costly because it meant that she had to continue with her education for much longer than she had previously expected, but by doing so, she went into a career that was far more suitable for her, and it was one that gave her a great deal of job satisfaction.

The alternative route would have been for Belinda to have continued and to have eventually qualified as a nutritionist. She was hard working and determined and would probably have crafted out a good career for herself. But, would she have been happy with her role?

Changing career direction happens quite a lot and it's hardly surprising considering that the decisions and options are made in such a short period of time and when we are so young. It's impossible for anyone to know whether they will stay in a certain role for life. But, it doesn't matter. Sometimes opportunities will arise that will take an individual off track but will provide a much more satisfying outcome. Errors can easily be rectified.

Sadly, many people stop at this point though, they become accepting of their lot. This is not self acceptance by the way, this is about being afraid to say, "I've made a mistake," or "I don't want to continue studying, I'll make do."

Getting to where you need to be may seem like an uphill struggle, but it's worth it, if the view from the top is amazing.

We've already discussed that setting goals is important and breaking down those goals into manageable stepping stones can make the whole process so much easier, but let me remind you that making these decisions is all about clarity of mind; it's about deciding what you really want in life and going after it wholeheartedly.

You may find, as did Belinda, that the end goal is not what you want at all, but don't consider this a failure, consider this an achievement in the progression that has been made and that the strength of your personality enabled you to say "I need to make some changes."

Your circumstances may dictate that you cannot go and retrain at college, but there are numerous ways to learn all the necessary skills for success or, to re-invent yourself so don't let that stop you. You can still study part-time, there are many evening classes that can be taken which can gain you the qualifications that you need to even enter college as a mature student later on if you so wish. There are always options.

It may be that qualifications are not the issue but perhaps, you lack experience. In this case, consider taking on a second job for a period of time during an evening or at the weekend. This isn't about working yourself towards exhaustion; this is about getting practical experience within the desired new role. Even if the work is not paid, you will be able to obtain fantastic feedback and recommendations from those that you have worked for.

This shows such courage and determination that it will open many doors.

There are opportunities for everyone irrespective of age. It is never too late to make important changes in life, to learn new qualifications, or to take on practical experience in a role which will highlight whether your chosen pathway is right for you.

Showing how much the goal is desired is one thing but it's important that you can communicate effectively when necessary and to be able to sell yourself so that you can give yourself a fighting chance to go into the work-stream that is right for you. It may be that you need to set-up your own business but don't really know where to start; all you have is an idea at this point.

Remember that a good idea is worth its weight in gold. Consider it, shape it and mould it and hold onto it, let that dream become even bigger and while you are doing so, you can gain the necessary qualifications or the practical experience that is necessary if you just put in that little extra effort.

Your dream is out there just waiting for you to put the necessary goals in place.

> 66 Put all excuses aside and remember
> this - you are capable. 99
> - Zig Ziglar -

Chapter 7
The Traits of Success

Success feels great. But the most important thing to remember is that anyone can have it if they set their minds towards it. It's knowing how to be successful that is the key. This means understanding all the principles of the journey that you have to make to enable yourself to make it big. Remember that it doesn't matter what line of work that you go into, it's not about your IQ, it's about your emotional intelligence, it's also about your ability to think clearly, to define your goals, and to go for them.

If you have someone in your life who has already achieved success then it's worth analysing their work methods. What is it about them that enable them to be successful?

- Is it their work ethics?
- Is it their determination?
- Is it their qualifications?
- Is it their creative drive?

Remember this, even the greats follow and replicate successful models. Steve Jobs attended meetings of the Homebrew Computer Club with Wozniak in 1975. He greatly admired Edwin H. Land, the inventor of instant photography and founder of Polaroid Corporation, and would explicitly model his own career after that of Land's (Wikipedia reference).

Analysing those around you makes for an interesting project. There is much that can be learned by observation. Most of us take others at face value; we see the outer layer, the parts of their personalities that they are willing to show. We don't necessarily get to know the real person. So when you analyse someone who is successful, you have to strip back the layers because no one is two-dimensional.

Let's consider your own character traits; if you listed all those vital components that equate to you "the person", you may be surprised as to how many layers you have. Consider this, when you meet people for the first time:

> What do you project when you meet someone socially?

> What do you project when you meet someone for the first time in a business sense?

You present yourself to that person and you do your utmost to appear friendly and professional and kind etc. But you're unlikely to show them every aspect that makes up your personality. It takes time for someone to get to know the real you.

So when you analyse a successful person, you have to bear this in mind. What you see initially is only one small aspect of their persona. So it takes time to really determine the core values and traits that lead to success. It's important to remember that you are not trying to copy them per se but merely wish to emulate the attributes that make for success.

If you can find yourself a mentor, this will enable you to learn much more quickly, because then you have the perfect opportunity to understand them and to ask questions and to establish their values priorities and beliefs too. Following on from your research, it's a good idea to make a list of your own values and beliefs which will form the strong foundations on which to start your journey towards wealth.

Remember that it's hard to see anyone's true reality underneath all the wrapping, but persevere because the secrets to their success will be there. They will have achieved their goals through discovering what works for them and they may have done this in a number of ways:

- Through their organisational skills
- Their creative skills
- By acting instinctively

It's only when you strip off the top layer that you can take a look at the reality of someone's life and see their progression and their behaviours.

A successful person will have a streamlined lifestyle and they will have very clear priorities and goals. They will only commit to those things that they believe in passionately. So therefore, an important lesson to learn is that you must eliminate as much clutter in life as possible. Otherwise, it becomes a distraction.

The inner millionaire represents people that are driven, they have a target in mind and they do everything they can to reach it. This means they have clear outcomes and they have considered their stepping stones towards success in advance. Importantly, they know what success looks like and they know what it feels like.

Most successful people have not become that way overnight. They've taken a slow but measured route towards achieving their goals. In essence, they diversify their income and maximise their assets. Those who have become wealthy in financial terms live within their means, and by this I mean that they are wise with their money. They may accumulate but they reinvest it wisely.

Important Steps to The Inner Millionaire

There is no doubt that developing good habits will set those foundations towards wealth creation. If you take a good look at how you live your life, how driven you are and compare it to how much time you waste, then you will be able to see the areas of your life that needs shaping up.

Take a good look at your life and then consider how you can manage your time and become more efficient:

- Perhaps you watch too much TV? In which case limit yourself to one or two hours of TV a day.
- If you are already working, what do you do in your lunch hour? Could you use this more effectively— perhaps for goal setting or following other money making opportunities?

Do you create goals? If you don't, you really should. Successful people are extremely goal orientated, and in fact many plan their schedules the night before so that they have very clear mindset when they wake up.

I always think that it's good to set a variety of goals that will lead towards the ultimate goal. Setting short term goals initially will help inspire you, because once you start achieving those goals, you will feel encouraged and gain confidence about achieving the end result. The goals should be measurable and realistic so plan yours on a daily, weekly, monthly and then yearly basis. Your goals might be difficult to achieve if you have not considered them fully, they should be measurable but not so easy that they mean very little. Remember the only limit to your success comes from you.

The inner millionaire mindset is always looking to improve and grow; do you find new ways in which to improve? If yes, then you are on the right track. Self-improvement isn't about giving yourself a hard time while analysing all those bad habits; instead, consider it a positive approach enabling you to fine-tune those aspects of your personality that may hold you back. For example, if you are driven by a fear of failure, then this underlining fear will impact everything that you do. You will be more cautious and analytic as opposed to trusting your gut instinct and your judgement.

If you want to be a successful business person and have all the wealth, health and happiness in your life, then you have to start taking care of yourself. Let's say you are setting up a new business, there is often a need you for you to invest long hours in the work-place, in which case making time for a nutritious diet and exercise would benefit you in the end because you will feel more energetic and able to cope.

Finding a balance in life is very important, if you can take a healthy approach to everything that you do, you will find life becomes easier, and ultimately more enjoyable. When you consider those successful people around you, note that they will have a very positive and dynamic outlook on life. They will be enthusiastic and energetic in their approach. Successful people don't think they are lucky to be successful. They expect to be successful because they deserve it to be this way. If you take these attributes on board, you need to see that obstacles are merely challenges and view those irritating problems as opportunities.

If you come from a less than positive background, it's very easy to fall back on old habits and to become less than positive yourself, but it's important that you don't reduce your opportunities for success by allowing any self-doubts or self limitations to scupper your plans. It can be all too easy to start feeling negatively, even more so if you are not looking after yourself in terms of diet and nutrition. Older learned behaviours can seemingly trip you up at every turn, so be very aware of your thought processes and nip any negativity in the bud before it becomes a problem.

When you start out on your chosen career path, inevitably there will be some tough times ahead. But it's important to never give up, always have hope and belief in your own abilities. But take a realistic approach to success too. If something is not working, don't be afraid to change it.

Spend time with professionals who also take a positive approach in life. You can learn much from other people who are striving towards success; similarly, if you spend time with those who are negative and who doubt their abilities at every turn, it will be all too easy for you to pick up the same negative habits. Don't give into fears, recognise what they are and then take a positive approach towards overcoming them.

You can learn a lot by listening, through discussion and by observing those around you. It's an interesting pastime to be able to discover the secrets of those fabulously wealthy and happy individuals who seem to have everything they want. But the message within this book has always been to confirm how easy it will be to achieve your dreams if you only put your mind to it. Rewire your mind for success. The most important aspect is to understand what you want in life and then, work out a plan of how to get there.

Throughout your day, your conscious and subconscious mind will be bombarded by images and random impressions, and when your head is filled with so much clutter, it's hard to analyse the route to success unless you can clear your mind. If you can learn and practice meditation, it will become easy to let go of all of your thoughts and to clear your mind totally. By doing so, you will embed the process towards relaxing at will and be able to clear your mind on command.

Analysing your journey is always useful and there is no doubt that your route to success will be littered with some difficult obstacles, but providing you are flexible in your approach, can adapt to situations while never taking your eyes off the end goal, and you can remain alert, you will get there. It's all about perseverance, developing good business habits, common sense and having a positive and energised attitude.

> 66 Rich people plan for 3 generations, poor people plan for Saturday night. 99
> - *Unknown* -

Mark Cuban is an American businessman, investor, and owner of the NBA's Dallas Mavericks, Landmark Theatres, and Magnolia Pictures, and the chairman of the HDTV cable network AXS TV. He is also a "shark" investor on the television series Shark Tank. In 2011, he was worth over 2.7 billion dollars.

What many people don't realise about Mark Cuban is that he wasn't born with a silver spoon in his mouth. In fact, his father was an automobile upholsterer and he grew up in a middle-class family. He didn't have the money to pay for college, so he held down whatever jobs he could find so he could pay his way—he even worked as a disco dance instructor.

Graduating from college, Cuban moved to Dallas, TX, and took a job as a bartender before becoming a salesman for one of the first software retailers in the city, earning him $18k per year plus commission. Mark didn't know much about computers but was certainly open and willing to learn. A persistent sales person, it wasn't long before Mark was given an opportunity to make a $15,000 sale, which in turn would earn him a $1,500 commission, the biggest pay day of his career to date. Fortunately, Mark was fired for disobeying the "do not sell" request to that account and that spark lit his entrepreneurial flame.

More people who are fired experience moderate depression, and don't return to full-time employment for a period of time. Not the case for 25 year old Mark Cuban, he responded by starting his own company. In fact, Mark went straight back to that account he'd sold, and used his contacts to convince the business owner to fund a start up called Micro-Solutions that grew into a company with $30M in revenue. That capital enabled him to fund AudioNet, and the rest, well, is history.

One of Cuban's cardinal rules for owning your business is: Don't start a business unless you love it. People spend countless hours working, and owning a business of course takes them away from friends and family. So it's best to love and enjoy what you do! (Wikipedia reference)

As you can see from the story above, Mark Cuban utilised his inner millionaire attributes and they helped him become a billionaire. Once again, he was someone who was prepared to do anything as a job without pride obstructing him, he wasn't born wealthy but had the hunger to create and negotiate with his ability to sell. He suffered many setbacks in life and was still able to go beyond his comfort zone and approach one of his clients to fund him in his business venture.

All successful people will tell you go after what you love, I believe it's time for people to start listening and acting.

Chapter 8

The Importance of Values

Most of your values will have been learned through your parent's guidance and in the main, once identified, they are likely to be relevant. But remember that we are talking about your values and it's important to not be influenced by others. It is fine to have different goals from those of your parents or from other family members or colleagues, your circumstances may be very different.

If you're not sure of your own values, you are doing yourself a disservice. If you are guilty of embracing the values of others—perhaps those in authority, such as your superiors or colleagues, perhaps even in society itself, then it's time to stop. Always remember that you are your own person and you can think for yourself. You can take up the mantle of work-place values but this does not mean dropping your own. Your values in life will be influenced frequently and perhaps unconsciously and as your life evolves, external influences will no doubt test some of your values.

In life, the strongest and most resilient succeed, so you need to know who you are and have a determined focus while being anchored in life. Remember that your actions as you strive forwards towards success may contradict sometimes with your beliefs and this means that there could be gaps between your behaviour and your values, leading to inner conflict. By being aware of the person that you are, of your vision and of your ultimate goals, you will be able to fill in the gaps and to lessen conflict.

So, now you know the importance of being able to define your own values in life, you may find it easier once you know exactly what they are in general terms. Consider your values to be the lynch pin that holds everything together in terms of how you live your life, and of course, how you plan your work remit too. This means that the values govern your priorities and you can measure your successes by those values too.

When you live your life in accordance to your values, you will usually feel a sense of contentment, life ticks along nicely. But when you ignore your values and the actions you take jar with those pre-decided values, things can suddenly start to feel wrong.

So from this you can see that it is important to identify and to live by your values. Values tend to fall into two categories:

Personal Life Value

These determine the most important values which can include time with your family and money etc.

Personal Job Content Objectives

These determine any required combination of skills which include: physical, creative and technical etc.

When you acknowledge your chosen values, life becomes so much easier. Everything slips into place and you are working in accordance to all that you believe in. Here's an example of where conflict can creep in surprisingly quickly:

If you are working in a job that does little by way of satisfying your inner goals and the hours are long and the schedule is demanding, then spending time away from your home, and all that you hold dear, might make you face inner conflict.

Sometimes we fall into our roles in life, not by choice, but just by circumstances, and if you find yourself in a role that does not appeal or that requires skill-sets that you don't have, you will simply feel pressured and unsatisfied. It will seem as if a piece of the puzzle is missing.

How to Define Your Values

Although it may seem difficult initially to create a list of values, a little forethought can soon help you to create a long list, however they will not all be relevant to you. So the hard part then can be in determining the values that represent you. It's important to also decide those that should be pushed to one side.

We have already said that values help to pave the way towards the future and help to create balance in your life so although most of the values that you come up with may represent you in some way, you have to be able to prioritise and to choose those values that are the most beneficial.

Here are some career-related values to give you a starting point:

- Personal development
- Leadership
- Loyalty
- Security
- Wealth
- Status
- Independence
- Power
- Integrity
- Effort

Personal values may include:

- Appreciation
- Caring
- Compassion
- Commitment
- Cooperation
- Courtesy
- Forgiveness
- Honesty
- Friendships

Once you start considering your personal values and defining them, you will find that it's a great way of being able to ascertain the important aspects of your life. For this next exercise, we are going to look back at your life so that you can consider those most positive times and to consider also aspects where you felt you made the right decisions.

Take your time with this because it is an important step towards your changing your life for good. Make a list of the times when you felt content or most happy. This can be in your personal life, your work life or, a combination of the two:

1.

2.

3.

4.

5.

Now, using your list, consider:

- What were you doing at those times?
- Who were you with?
- Were you happy as a result of the decisions that you made?

List the times in your life when you have felt proud of your achievements—this can be personally and professionally.

- What happened to make you proud?
- Consider the factors that contributed to those feelings and list in order?

How were your values connected with your achievements?

1.

2.

3.

You can use your values in all areas of your life, they can guide you like a moral compass emotionally and physically. When your decisions and your values are in sync, you will be able to go forward with confidence. The types of questions you can ask are:

- What career path should I be on?
- Is it time to set up my new business? Am I ready?
- Should I change my career?

Bear in mind that your values might change as you go through life. Although your values will usually be stable, some values will become a priority and others may lessen. When you are striving to create your successes in life, you may well find that the values associated with finances are more important, but once you have achieved certain goals, your values may alternate and values relating to family will become much more recognised.

The next step is to prioritise your values in life but in the first instance, work on just creating a list and try to include everything. You can amend and delete any entries later. Once you have done so, select them in order of priority. This may be difficult initially and it may help to have a target focus in mind.

Your values should be re-evaluated regularly to make sure that they continue to fit well with your life. Don't forget that your values are not just about the here and now but about your future too.

Answer the following questions to confirm that you understand the importance of your values:

- Consider the top 3 values, are you proud of them?
- If asked, would you be happy to share this information with others?
- Will your values help you to achieve your current goals?
- Do your values make you feel good about yourself and your goals?

These values are an integral part of you. They provide the foundations upon which your life is set. It's important to keep this in mind. If you consider that the choices you make in life are often about doing what is best for you and, the goals represent something of value to you. If your preset values are strong, they provide you with an accurate guiding principle and you can rely on them throughout your journey to success.

In addition to listing your top values, also consider those that you would be willing to give up or to push to one side. List the bottom three below:

1.

2.

3.

Now lists the three lower values that you would **be least** willing to give up:

1.

2.

3.

Your values are your principles but they can and will change. Nothing is ever set in stone. There will be times when you reflect on your values and find that instinctively they have grown as you have. This isn't a bad thing; in fact, it's often good to have a reminder of your personal growth. What was important once is no longer, it's like the ebb and flow of the tide, you take a flexible approach to your priority values but always use them keep them in mind and act accordingly. This attitude will help to aide your journey.

> 66 It's not hard to make decisions once you know
> what your values are. 99
> - Roy. E. Disney -

Chapter 9

The Laws of Wealth and Your Relationship With Money

Write down what you think money can do for you. It's your true feelings that count here.

One of my student's gave me a classic example to the definition of money.

"Money is so hard."

Petra admitted that she found it difficult to make money so I said to her:

"I want you to go back and to think about a specific incident in your life where you felt money was really difficult."

She said initially she couldn't think of a time but after a few attempts she came up with a story without her even noticing. She told me in her early 20s, she had been a model and in the modelling world, agencies don't pay really well, she worked extremely long hours and had never received a promotion or a pay rise.

Then one day a new model came and told the agency that she would not work for them unless she was paid a much higher amount than everybody else, and she got it. This didn't just happen once but numerous times. Petra witnessed this and couldn't believe it.

So she thought she would do the same but this time, the boss said no to her pay rise and as a result, she had experienced a strong sense of rejection resulting in her relationship with money becoming tainted.

Now this was not her only bad experience, but the problem is that once this perception was formed, it almost certainly sabotaged future earning deals. In my teachings, I show people how to change that mindset and give them specific strategies to ensure they get paid what they are worth.

What most people haven't realised is that there is a massive difference between thinking and feeling. When it comes to making decisions in life, people don't do what they think, they do what they feel.

I'll explain.

People think about money in a positive way but the way they feel about money is often negative. Since we are governed by our feelings, this explains why most people never earn the riches they deserve.

The conscious mind controls the way you think about things and your subconscious mind controls the way you feel so people need to reprogram or rewire their mind if they have any chance to reach financial freedom.

This is what causes frustration and procrastination when the subconscious mind isn't congruent with the conscious mind; many people get opportunities in life and you always hear this reason when someone has failed to seize the opportunity—"It didn't feel right".

Even though the opportunity could have made complete sense.

The three ways we are conditioned:

What did we hear about money growing up?

"Money is the root of all evil."

"Money doesn't grow on trees."

How did we see our parents handle money?

- Were your parents fearful of money?
- Did they consistently fight?
- Were they risk takers?
- Were they spenders?
- Were they savers and scared to invest?

The fact is we become at least one of our parents in how we deal with money, unless we recognise the importance of becoming the complete opposite in order to create wealth.

What experiences have you seen because of money?

- Did you experience divorces over money?
- Did you feel a lot of stress?
- Did dad control all the money in the household?
- This is how we start to form our relationship and perception of money.

The Laws to the Money Matrix

What you pay yourself first, is for you to keep.

People who do not manage what they earn will end up living pay cheque to pay cheque. They are reliant on their good health to ensure employment in later years, without considering that eventually hard work will not be maintained.

Savings is your foundation for the future; they represent financial security and your belief in yourself. This wealth will support your future living. The key is to allow your money to work hard for you.

Without savings for the future, people start to stress and live without certainty. People cannot live their dreams and are burdened by thoughts of what it might have been.

What You Pay Yourself Makes You Rich

There is a myth that in order to save you need to earn a lot of money. It has nothing to do with how much you earn, it's all about developing the HABIT of managing your money, having a system in place, if you can't manage a little a bit of money then you won't be able to manage a large portion. How much you save will determine your wealth. There are always stories of high earners who have spent money as quickly as they have made it, or those lottery winners, who have lost their prize in a short period of time. Wealth is determined by 3 things: the ability to save it, make it, and keep it.

Those that can save will build their self-esteem and are held in high regard by their loved ones because they have security. What you pay yourself forms those future investments that will make you rich.

The Principles Shall Never Be Diminished

The principle must be a safe and low risk; you must ensure you are expecting a fair and reasonable growth without putting your principle at high risk.

Those who risk more than they can afford and who live beyond their means have robbed themselves of any chance of contentment and peace of mind. Your savings and income must be divided for long term returns, but also have a portion dedicated to higher risk returns. 90% of the world's population endure hardship and struggle. This one rule will change your financial future and steer you on the path of security and independence.

Hide Your Savings From Temptation

Those who care about their futures will invest in products or services that appreciate in value, and those you don't care about themselves will invest in products or services that depreciate in value (as quoted by Dr. John DeMartini). Your savings are everything, and stand between you and a life of pain. I do believe people should spoil themselves as a reward of their achievements, however we must ensure that our rewards do not exceed the growth of our wealth.

A lot of people spend money on their image to impress others and this is why self-love is so important, as it will stop you spending needlessly on things that will not give you anything in return, other than short term pleasure.

Money is attracted to whom best can manage it.

"A wise man can manage money but a fool cannot."

60% of the world's population are financially poor and will struggle in most areas of their life.

30% of the population become content and get stuck in a comfort zone, even though they struggle financially and have some perceived level of success. The remaining 10% are rich and wealthy, and enjoy abundance throughout their lives for they know how to grow and manage their wealth.

"Those who cannot control their emotions, cannot create great wealth."

Those that seek to grow their wealth come from a place of power and are not driven by fear or greed, they commit to a system, a plan of surgical precession which creates sustainable financial growth.

Those who deviate do so by falling victim to temptation, greed, pride, envy, apathy and self-righteousness.

Negative emotions are the Achilles' heel of financial struggle and they will pull you from a life of true financial independence. People must decouple their emotion to money and plan on creating wealth for generations, where most people plan for their weekend and for easy short-term pleasures, not appreciating that life will be harder on them later.

No one will pay you more than you think you are worth

The image and definition that you have created is the tapestry of your life. This wealth index is your current reality and defines everything about you, what you do and how you do it.

This wealth index was your creation and no one else, you are the game setter of your life and you will determine your worth to others. Learn the art of interaction and don't fall into a comfort zone. Your comfort zone will determine your worth in the market.

Those who can change their definition or self image of themselves will change their blueprint, which in turn changes their reality. Self belief will allow you to deserve more abundance in your life and to get it.

It is not your employer or clients who pay you, it is you.

The employer or client pays you what you think you are worth. In reality, it is you who determines your price in the market and your belief in what you can achieve and do is based on your own level of self worth. Most people are afraid to ask for what they are worth and this is due to the lack of confidence and self esteem that they perceive in themselves.

Employers and your clients are consistently looking for people to exceed their expectations but the question is, will that be you? People love to be served and given value on their investments. Position yourself from a place of value because if you value yourself, the world will value you too.

Those who do what inspires them get paid for what they love and do not feel they are working

People who have found their true purpose or mission in life will always be inspired and happy. They do not need to be motivated or rely on the alarm clock to wake them up. They are living a life that is congruent with their inner purpose.

I have always said it makes sense to get paid doing what you love or to learn to love what you do. You should never feel you are working or become a prisoner of the system.

Focus on what you want in life and allow your labour to pay for it.

What the most challenged see as problems, the rich see as opportunities.

The rich live in the opportunity and solution world, where as the challenged see the problems and downside in every opportunity that comes their way. The rich understand that problems are great things because without problems, there are no opportunities. If you want to start a business in life, my advice would be: don't look for a business but seek out a problem in our world and then provide the world with a solution, and that's where you now you have a business.

"The poor will succumb to problems; the rich will rise."

Those that serve others, serve themselves.

True fulfilment stems from the moment you hear thank you. It's that moment when you know you have created an act of service. I believe if you serve the world, the world will serve you. Wealth is created in the act of service; it is in the exchange of goods and services.

The higher the value in service, the more exchange you will receive and the wealthier you will become.

Rich people focus on the big picture, their vision is simply an act of service to the world and their lives of fulfilment, happiness and abundance is created in the act of service.

Rule your mind or it will rule you.

Summary

Congratulations on reaching this part of the book, I hope you have found it informative, instructional and thought-provoking. Think of it as a guideline to help you to analyse your current standing in life and to enable you to blaze a trail forward so that you can achieve all of your goals.

The ethos of this book has always been on how to release your inner millionaire and it's important to remember that anyone can free their potential to be able to achieve all the wealth that they desire. They just have to shrug off any negative pre-learned behaviour which can limit their growth and to start believing in themselves.

Remember those universal fitness attributes? By achieving all of these attributes in your life, you will be successful and have a balanced approach to life:

- Emotional fitness
- Mental fitness
- Spiritual fitness
- Financial fitness

Wealth equals empowerment and it provides you with so many options in life including:

- Freedom
- Flexibility
- Recourse
- Opportunities, etc.

True wealth is about having a vision for the future and to then be able to manifest any desires so that they become tangible entities. Wealth creation encompasses every aspect of your life and so understanding your association with money, and the important areas within your career and personal life, you will be able to have all of the things you covet the most. It sounds simple and in principle it really is.

Let me just remind you:

- You need clarity of mind
- You need to set goals
- You must banish negativity
- You need to embrace a positive approach to life
- You need to discover your values and live by them

Everything that is laid out in this book is absolutely true. If you want to change your life for the better, simply work your way through it and absorb the message within. Don't just read it though, do something about it. Put all the knowledge you have to good use and never, ever give up. You have the power to change every aspect of your life and to greet each day with a smile, having achieved all that you dream of.

Your story may take time to develop. It may require you to amend and rethink your goals and your actions. You may need to be flexible in your approach; you may need to stand strong. The end result will depend upon where you are in your life currently and how big your goals are. But don't settle for smaller goals because it's easier.

Reach for those true aspirations because you really do deserve to be successful.

If you have enjoyed this book, take a look at Andrew Barsa's website for more information.

About the Author

A ndrew Barsa is the creator of the financial wealth mindset program, *The Inner Millionaire*. Over the years, he has associated with some of the richest and most challenged people in the world. His biggest question was, "Why do some people become wealthy, and others do not?"

Andrew quickly eliminated the usual reasons that most people give: family, background, connections, skill set, education and so on. None of these factors actually made a difference. He met educated and gifted people who were barely making ends meet, and at the same time, he was baffled how the uneducated and unfortunate became highly successful.

After a while, Andrew began to realise something very important: most people actually have the amount of money they truly believe they are worth.

"What it boils down to is this," he says. "Financial struggle is actually a state of mind. It's the sum total of all the little stories we tell ourselves."

With this realisation, he began to listen to what people were saying about money and to understand their relationship to it.

Andrew believes, "We all have an inner gift."

Born in Sydney to immigrant parents, life was tough for Andrew and his family. His formative memories were of a constant financial battle as his parents struggled to provide for their family. It was during his studies of business management that he became most disillusioned, having overheard his lecturer stressing about money, and seeing him leave in an old, worthless car. He thought to himself, "Is this the educational system I'm learning from?" He made a decision from that moment on to surround himself with successful mentors.

Feeling worthy of becoming successful, he thought, "If they can do it, so can I." Coincidentally his fears of failure diminished as his accomplishments grew.

His first job was data entry; from there he moved into the property sector and finally found his calling by surrounding himself with successful traders. The time spent in the financial markets became the major turning point in his life and ignited a passion for wealth psychology.

For a period of several years Andrew dedicated himself to the research and understanding of the underlying influences which occur in successful minds. What he discovered was that it does not matter what avenue you take in life. Whether it is as an entrepreneur, a property guru or, successful investor, having the IQ and knowledge is one thing, however the EQ (emotional quotient or intelligence) is what really matters. The ability to identify, understand and manage emotions in positive ways is paramount. To make wise, financial decisions you have to know how to relieve stress, communicate effectively, to empathise with others, to overcome challenges, and to defuse conflict. EQ is about mastering your inner blue print, allowing you to live a successful life in any field.

Andrew says, "Knowledge will give you education but success is the program of the mind."

During this time he observed patterns and developed a successful unique formula, which he has taught in his seminars and through various pieces of literature.

Andrew Barsa has been invited to speak on the global stage alongside Sir Richard Branson, James Caan, Mark Bouris, and Facebook's Randi Zuckerberg, Dr John DeMartini, Co-Founder of Apple Steve Wozniak and many others on the mindset of success and how to produce immediate results for businesses and individuals. Those who have applied his proven method have experienced life-altering changes.

9780099419299 8